WRITING DOWN THE VISION

ALSO BY KEI MILLER

Poetry

Kingdom of Empty Bellies
There is an Anger that Moves
Light Song of Light
The Cartographer Tries to Map a Way to Zion (forthcoming)

Fiction

The Fear of Stones and Other Stories
The Same Earth
The Last Warner Woman

Edited

New Caribbean Poetry: An Anthology

KEI MILLER

WRITING DOWN THE VISION
ESSAYS & PROPHECIES

PEEPAL TREE

First published in Great Britain in 2013
Peepal Tree Press Ltd
17 King's Avenue
Leeds LS6 1QS
England

ISBN13: 9781845232283

Supported using public funding by
ARTS COUNCIL
ENGLAND

CONTENTS

Write down the vision and make it plain, so that he who readeth may run.

– from The Book of Habakkuk

INTRODUCTION AND ACKNOWLEDGEMENTS

My first book was a collection of short stories and it has occasionally baffled me that I have never returned to that genre. Looking at the pieces gathered here, I see now that I never left it. In a sense these are short stories even if they can't be called "short-fiction". The exception is the earliest piece collected here "A Kind of Silence", but even this short story, towards its end, moves into a nonfictional mode.

There are those who say the short story is a natural genre for Caribbean writers but I find that argument a little patronizing. Proponents of the view say it is something about oral cultures and stories told by firesides and wise grandmothers and Anansi, and how all these things lend themselves to short rather than long fiction. Now there might actually be some truth to all of that, but I rather think that the Caribbean's gravitation towards shorter pieces has to do with time and resources and publishing houses – things which writers of long fiction need to sustain their craft, and to which Caribbean writers have not had ready access. Instead we have written pieces that can fit inside newspapers or magazines or whatever small space has been offered us.

The pieces collected here were written in a variety of places – the earliest in Jamaica, a couple in Iowa, some in Glasgow, one in the Philippines, and so on. Two of these essays were posts on my blog. They are products of movement and migration, as obsessed with the Caribbean as with what it means to live and write away from home.

If on one hand these essays embrace narrative and exist on the border of the fictional "short story", on the other hand they embrace polemic and exist on the border of prophecy. I imagine these as the sounds a man might make who has been living out in the wilderness, trying sometimes to shout and sometimes to whisper to the world in

which he lives. As a collection, these represent something of my vision of the Caribbean seen from up-close and sometimes from afar, a vision I have been obsessed with writing down.

They are mostly occasional pieces, written on request for particular events or in response to particular situations. To those magazine editors and newspaper editors and conference organizers who made these requests, I would like to say thanks. So often, we are not short of things to say; we are only short of the spaces (however small) in which to say them.

- "The Texture of Fiction" originally appeared in *The Edinburgh Review*.
- "These Islands of Love and Hate" originally appeared in *The Glasgow Herald*.
- "A Kind of Silence" originally appeared in the anthology *Moving Right Along: Caribbean Stories in Honour of John Cropper*.
- A larger essay, "The Art of Tongues, the Craft of Prophecy" eventually downsized itself to the current "The Women Who Carried Pencils behind their Ears" and originally appeared in *PN Review*.
- "A Smaller Song" was originally part of a presentation as the Bridget Jones Travel Bursary recipient at the Society of Caribbean Studies Conference. It subsequently appeared in my collection *A Light Song of Light*.
- "But in Glasgow, There are Plantains" originally appeared in *The International Journal of Scottish Literature*.
- "Imagining Nations" originally appeared in *Moving Worlds*.
- "Writing with Elephants" appeared first in *Newbooks Magazine*.
- "The Grief Spaces" was a commissioned travel essay for the US State Department.
- "A Smaller Sound, a Lesser Fury – a Eulogy for Dub Poetry" was a presentation at the Scottish Universities International Summer School.
- "Maybe Bellywoman Was on di Tape" was originally a keynote address at the Shadows and Shorelines conference at the University of Reading.
- "The Spaces between Poems" was a commissioned piece for

the National Association of Literature Development's Spring
conference "The Spaces Between Us".
- "In Defence of Maas Joe" and "An Occasionally Dangerous
 Thing Called 'Nuance'" were originally posted as blogs on
 my website, keimiller.wordpress.com.

THE WOMEN WHO CARRIED PENCILS BEHIND THEIR EARS
(2007/2012)

Every writer is asked the same question over and over – who are the other writers that have influenced you the most? Put like that, the answers are easy enough for me: Lorna Goodison, Emily Dickinson, David Malouf, Kamau Brathwaite, for starters. But I think, better put, the question would be more amorphous – something like "who are the people or what are some of the things that have shaped your voice?" Then our answers wouldn't be so easy. We would have to think through a more complicated genealogy that included songs, movies, grandparents, radio hosts, snippets of overheard speech. In my case it would include a few preachers and prophets, and also a wall.

There is Sister Gilzene – a thin elderly woman from the starch-stiff church I used to go to as a child, and whose eruptions of tongues into the sobriety of Sunday morning service was always smoothed away by a deacon, as if the old woman's glossolalia existed in the creases of her purple frock – as if it was coming from her bunched shoulders and not from her mouth.

My genealogy would include Sister Sybil as well, another old woman, though larger in size than Gilzene. Hers was a great expanse of breasts and body and sound. She belonged to another church – the one I escaped to, before I escaped church altogether. It was a church that made space for eruptions, and when I used to go there, Sister Sybil's uninterrupted tongues always had in it the resonance of thunder and the music of rain.

Sister Sybil has even made cameo appearances in my work. Sometimes by name:

Whenever Sister Sybil raise the red banner
the air change, the tempo change, the mood

change, and inside that place, God
begins to happen.[1]

And sometimes by image alone:

Because of her mountain breasts
she has learnt a peculiar walk, a duck-stride
to balance herself. It is hard to see anything
but the stern shifting of those mountains
when in flat, battleship shoes
she marches across the aisle.[2]

Sister Sybil had a talking parrot – maybe it is still alive – a vicious green thing who would demand peanuts then snap at your fingers. Strange the way she seemed to gift everything around her with language. Perhaps then Sybil, as in sibilant, or at a stretch, syllables. She was neither lovely nor lovable. She believed only in her God and the wretchedness of all mankind. I avoided her because even back then I never looked the part of a good Christian boy. My dreadlocks were particularly offensive. Whenever Sister Sybil spotted me she would try to lay heavy hands on my hair and pray.

It was Sister Sybil who once said to my friend when she was barely an eleven-year old girl, "Child! Me and de devil was fighting for yu soul last night!" Apocalyptic drama queen. She walked off after that, withholding from my friend the answer to the question that would haunt her for years – "Who won?"

My genealogy would include some whose names I have never known, like the bus preachers who would climb up onto the number 75 buses at Half-Way-Tree, their sermons lasting at least the five miles to Papine where I, caught up in their cadences, would have to reluctantly disembark. I remember one in particular who, in rebuking a woman for her less-than-noble career, accused her of dancing on tables and in skirts so short that he was able to see right up into her "birth-ina" – and it was this soldering together of words (not his condemnation) that made me appreciate that he was a wordsmith and that I belonged to his tribe.

My genealogy would have to include – most bizarrely – a concrete wall which despite its proximity to the sea and to salty air seemed never in danger of crumbling. In fact, this was a growing wall. The man who was forever adding to its height was quite clearly deranged.

He wrote urgent messages onto the wall, hoping perhaps that the government or at least his neighbours would one day read them and heed his warnings. On Sunday evenings my father used to drive us out to Port Henderson for fried fish and bammy, and on the way back we would drive very slowly by this wall, and although we used to laugh, I think secretly we also found it beautiful. It was why we kept coming back. And it was something of a loss when the government really did seem to read it, or took notice of its height which broke every town planning rule and regulation, and so ordered it destroyed.

And the church women of my youth (Sister Gilzene and Sister Sybil), and the bus preachers on the number 75 bus, and that ever-growing wall, all belong to yet another genealogy. Each one of them, in their own way, is descended from a family of Jamaican "warner women", those prophetesses of doom who used to carry pencils behind their ears. The pencils were supposed to represent a readiness to receive heavenly messages. Warner women would then pass on these messages to earthly citizens. Warner women connected the immediate worlds around them to what they understood was a larger truth.

Warner women would never confess to what I now understand is a complicated and a learned aesthetic – a careful craft of prophecy, a meditated art of speaking in tongues. One is not supposed to admit to artistry in what is supposed to be divinely inspired. And yet it is as much the art of these women, as it is that of Emily Dickinson, David Malouf and Lorna Goodison, that shapes my voice.

From the women who carried pencils behind their ears I learn that one is allowed to speak without irony – that most favoured mode of Western (and particularly British) writers, as if its use is the only way to signal a sharp and a nuanced intelligence, as if we have to always undercut the things we say and the things we most deeply believe in, lest we be accused of being precious or earnest. From the women who carried pencils behind their ears, I learn that it is okay to be loud and exclamatory, that power doesn't always come from restraint and quietness, that sometimes power comes from power, and that some things are worth shouting about. From the women who carried pencils behind their ears I learn how to hold on to grief and onto myself and how to tremble at the strain. From them I even learn the use of metaphors – moons sinking in blood, alligators unable to walk

on roads, as if to say – if you're going to draw for the impossible, then make your imagination wide. Sometimes, it's as if I have inherited their pencils and have begun to write down their visions.

End Note

1. "Church Women: War Dance", *Kingdom of Empty Bellies* (Coventry: Heaventree Press, 2005), p. 22.
2. "Church Women: Mother", *Kingdom of Empty Bellies*, p. 12

THE TEXTURE OF FICTION
(2007)

"It always amuses me that the biggest praise for my work comes for the imagination, while the truth is that there's not a single line in all my work that does not have a basis in reality. The problem is that Caribbean reality resembles the wildest imagination."
— Gabriel Garcia Marquez

I would like to offer you a rosary of stories in no particular order or scheme – all of them true, and about the place where I am from. I am from the Caribbean which is, incidentally, a much better thing to say than this other thing that has become popular: I am from the islands. "The islands" seem to me a phrase robbed of any geo-political or historical substance, a shell of a term offered so that the hearer, if not from our quaint and nebulous island (whether it be St Kitts, the Philippines, or Hawaii) can throw imaginary garlands of hibiscuses around our necks, imbuing us with all kinds of exotic baggage, and license and forgiveness. So I am from the Caribbean, and if you are not from there then the stories I tell you now might not make immediate sense. Or you might think I'm lying, or perhaps exaggerating. Sometimes Caribbean logic is its own.

In 2005 there was a woman who was killed twice – the second time at her own funeral. On the first occasion of her death it had been of natural causes. At her funeral the family gathered in large numbers, dressed in black or purple, with hymns in their mouths. But in the middle of tears and slow organ music, there was the sudden explosion of gunshots. Not a gun-salute; a gang war had broken out in the community around them, and then a bullet entered the church. I narrate this slowly, as if the bullet had politely opened the church door, took off its hat, apologized

for interrupting and stated the nature of his business. Obviously this was not the case. It rudely shattered through the stained glass window, splintered through the closed coffin, and found its way into the heart of the dead woman, as if being an agent of death it was drawn immediately to the one life that wasn't. Surprisingly, no one seemed thankful for the dead woman's heroic act – how in pulling the bullet into herself she had likely been someone's salvation. Instead the mourners complained at the injustice of the gang, their insensitivity towards the corpse – that being dead already there was no need for the bullet to make it unambiguous – and how the handsome coffin they had spent good money on was now ruined.

Recently, in my own country, we had a plague of baby crabs. It happened in the parish of St Thomas, in a seaside community. Everyone had gone to bed as usual but woke up during the night when they felt aggressive insects crawling onto their beds and over their feet, or dropping from the ceiling and into their open, snoring mouths. Imagine the spluttering and the flailing arms. Imagine the frantic lights being turned on everywhere until they discovered the tiniest of crabs, thousands and thousands of them, coming in with the moon tide, scuttling into the houses, covering all the surfaces. Doors were flung open and men, women and children ran. That night the whole community huddled on the road, a little distance away from their homes, some of them crying, most of them praying, looking anxiously to the sky to see if God was coming. God did not come, but the sun did, and with its early morning beams all the baby crabs, still scurrying around, were smitten dead. Only then could people return to their houses, rake the remnants of the plague out of their yards and back into the Caribbean sea which had brought them.

There is a haunted house in Guyana that has made me believe in the devil. In truth, I only saw the foundations of this house, because on the day that I got there, it was a week too late. Despite earnest protestations from the community, the house had been demolished. This was a humble peasant's house, by the way, not the sprawling gothic mansion of similar American folklore. The

first occupants had been a rice farmer, his wife and their three children. They lived, I imagine, in relative domestic happiness and turmoil. Then one night, the rice farmer decided it was a good idea to go to the room of his two older children and kill them. He went back to his own room and killed the baby, then his wife and then himself. In every world, in every language, this is a tragedy. So there was shock and there was mourning, and then a year had passed. The year passed and the house became simply what we call, a "dead-lef", an inheritance waiting to be claimed. Into it moved a cousin of the rice farmer with his own wife and his own two children. They lived in that house in relative domestic happiness and turmoil, until one night the cousin went from room to room, killed his two children, then his wife, then himself. There was shock and there was mourning, and then a year had passed. Another relative moved into this tragic house, lived there for a year with his wife and three children. You know their destiny. One night the man grabbed his cutlass and with much splashing of blood ended the lives of his three children and his wife and himself. In all fourteen people were slaughtered in that house. Eleven murders and three suicides. And if you want to hold stubbornly to the epistemology that makes no allowance for spiritual dimensions, if you want to insist that this was merely a case of madness running in the family, then I might have asked you, months ago, to move into that house with your spouse and your two children. The community in Guyana knew better. They knew that this had something to do with evil, and with a world we cannot always see or smell or touch. I call it the devil, and the community knew he lived in that house which is why they insisted it not be destroyed – not because they wanted evil as their neighbour, but because at least it was contained. To destroy the house was to send the devil back into the world, like a roaring lion, seeking out whom he might devour. When I got there it was too late. The devil had been released.

I remember a tree in Jamaica that bore as its fruit, prophecies. That's what it seemed like to me. The tree was in a dust bowl right outside of my high school and there must have been a man or woman who used charcoal to write words like "Repent" or

"The Prime Minister must fall" or "Know ye this day who you shall serve" on squares of cardboard. These cardboard signs were hung up in the tree, and the branches had become overburdened with them, like a mango tree in season. Sometimes the wind would rattle these words, and the cardboards would hit against each other, such a strange and terrible sound, as if angels were crowded together, back to back, and were beating their wings.

I should I tell you about Queen Elizabeth II who came to Jamaica recently, and how in preparing for her arrival the government thought they should clean the city streets of litter, dog shit and dirt – and also of mad people. Maybe they thought they were being thorough because mad people were a combination of litter, dog shit and dirt. They rounded them up from around the city, put them in a truck and drove them miles and miles away, eventually dumping them by the edge of a poisonous lake, hoping, no doubt, that they would go for a swim and drown themselves. I do not know whether to prophesy with charcoal and cardboard the downfall of a government that could organize such a thing, or to praise the incredible distances that those women and men were able to walk, and the clear and precise sanity of their radars, so that one by one they found their way back to Kingston, in grand evening gowns of filth, ready to curtsy for the queen. Her royal highness's arrival was greeted by another small scandal – a power-cut at the house of the Governor-General. It was not so much the power-cut that was scandalous, but that the generators failed to chip in. Still, many thought this was fair, because on that night the queen, like everyone else in Jamaica, had to eat her rice and peas in darkness.

I will end with a story that makes me sad even now. Earlier this year, I saw a friend who seemed almost unreasonably happy. I commented on his joy, his buoyancy, and he said it was true – he was putting himself in a good mood because he had to, because the day had been such a horrible one. He told me that he knew it was going to be a horrible day because he woke to the news, broadcast over the radio, of a family from an inner-city community who had been burnt out of their houses. My friend works with an agency that lends support to families who, by some misfortune,

are suddenly without homes – so hearing the news that morning he was prepared for a hard day ahead. And yet, he wasn't. The news he heard when he entered his office and I will tell you now – and also tell you that this slight correction of the details has not been broadcast on any radio station in Jamaica – has not been written in any newspaper, because this story is not newsworthy.

The family was not exactly a family. It was a house of four young men who the community suddenly suspected were gay. They gave them only an hour to leave – to grab whatever they could and then turn their backs on what had been their home. There interposes this sad and simple law of physics: they could only take with them what they could carry. In sixty minutes how can anyone take complete stock, how can anyone consider carefully and rationally the inventory of his life? An important certificate will be left hanging on the wall, a crucial receipt will be forgotten in a pants' pocket, a fat envelope of money and a passport still in a drawer, incriminating evidence embarrassingly left under a mattress, life-saving tablets and a pre-scription still sitting on the night stand, a book of phone numbers on a table. How overwhelming it must be, the impulse to turn around, even to risk turning oneself into salt. Something that was left behind did bring one of the men back, and the community was waiting. They held him. They placed long rods of iron into the bonfire that had only recently been the house he lived in and then pressed these sizzling pieces of metal into his dark skin, burning through to pink soft mush, burning him until he collapsed. And though in this branding there were no actual words left on his ruined skin, every scar he now wears says: *Faggot. Battyman. Sodomite. Leave!*

If you ask me why I write stories, or novels, or poems, I would tell you it is because things that are real in my country, things that are factual, things that have happened and that continue to happen, have always had for me the quality of the unreal – the texture of fiction. This is what happens when you live in a country that is not the centre of the world; you become blessed with a kind of double vision. You see your life from the inside, and also from the outside – both locally and globally. You are conscious always of the reality of what you are living, and also the strange narrative of it. You become conscious of how this might be

observed – sometimes unlovingly and without empathy – if you do not find a way to tell it right. In a way, this is how every writer the world over lives – this quality of being inside and outside at the same time – of living a life while floating above it, observing, taking notes. Often times I find there is no need to invent or to create. There is only the need to see, and then to tell.

IN DEFENCE OF MAAS JOE
(2013)

Caribbean writing and Caribbean writers have come full circle – to the interesting place where we seem in danger of standing against many of the things we once stood for. For remember we are those whose project was once simple and noble: to challenge various centres of power. By writing in patois, we challenged orthodoxies of language; by writing about obeah or voodoo or in the mode of magic realism, we challenged orthodoxies of belief. Yes, that was us. Standing there on the outside, on the periphery as it were, we knew how to recognize and then challenge the dangerous cultural hegemonies of elite society. But to do that – to mount such a challenge – we had to privilege the folk and folk culture. We had to privilege people like Maas Joe and the story, perhaps, of his hapless donkey. And it's true (of course it is true) that such stories became too easy too quickly for too many of us. It became easy, especially for our less ambitious writers. We who were against orthodoxies had inadvertently created our own – a Caribbean orthodoxy. And so, in the very spirit of what our literature has been, we had to turn around and challenge ourselves. It is therefore not the challenge that I query right now. That is as it should be. I wonder, though, about the fervency of it. These days I begin to wonder if the pendulum hasn't swung too far; if our best writers are now too invested in writing about everyone else BUT Maas Joe and his rural life. We worry that we might be seen as trite and nostalgic. A new motto seems to hang over the desk of the modern Caribbean writer, a chant borrowed from rowdy political rallies that try to unseat incumbents: Maas Joe got to go.

The campaign against Maas Joe isn't at all new. David Dabydeen wrote in 1990:

The pressure now is towards mimicry. Either you drop the epithet "black" and think of yourself as a "writer" (a few of us foolishly embrace this position, desirous of the status of "writing" and knowing that "black" is blighted) – that is, you cease dwelling on the nigger/tribal/nationalistic theme, you cease *folking* up the literature, and you become "universal" – or else you perish in the backwater of small presses, you don't get published by the "quality" presses, and you don't receive the corresponding patronage of media-hype.[1]

And it isn't confined to Caribbean literature. Avarind Adiga's Booker Prize winning novel, *The White Tiger*, was praised almost rapturously by the *Sunday Times*. "Unlike almost any other Indian novel you might have read… this page-turner offers a completely bald, angry, unadorned portrait of the country as seen from the bottom of the heap; there's not a sniff of saffron or a swirl of sari anywhere." There is merit to both Adiga's novel and this review, for what I think is being critiqued here is not "the folk" per se but the "folksiness" that often surrounds them. This reviewer is interested in a perspective from those at "the bottom of the heap" but seems worried that the overused tropes of Indianness (and perhaps, by extension, the tropes of any national identity) can become a limiting place in which the folk are too often trapped. It is true that those who don't write their own stories – who become subjects of the writer's imagination – are often made to live in a nostalgic and simplistic world rather than the more complicated grit of what would be their more realistic lives. The novel simplifies lives of course, but maybe some lives are more simplified than others. I agree wholeheartedly then that the citizens of the developing world ought to be allowed to live modern, urban, and even Western lives in fiction, but I disagree that only such lives are authentic, or that the so-called simple life cannot and has not been depicted in all its stunning complexity. Can we not allow the folk to hold an iPad in one hand, and a mango in the other?

The growing campaign against saffron, saris, mangoes, obeah and Maas Joe's donkey, leads ultimately to our impoverishment. Recently I had to go to a fairly prominent high school in Jamaica to talk about literature and writing. I asked the students if they read Jamaican or Caribbean novels. A pall of silence fell on the group. One brave girl finally put up her hand and tried to explain. She hemmed and hawed, trying to get the words out. I think she knew that what she was about

to say would be politically incorrect, but nonetheless it was her truth and indeed the truth of the class.

"Caribbean literature doesn't really relate to us," she said. "And you know… it's like… I know people speak in patois and all of that, but you know, that's not how I speak. And so all these books are written in patois and it's like about slavery and all of that, and it's like, I just can't relate. You know what I mean?"

I have always found it a strange, and even a grossly unfair critique, to demand of fiction that it be real – that it be a direct reflection of our lives RIGHT NOW, that it have "literal" rather than "literary" merit. Did she really want a story about a middle-class girl in Jamaica, who lived in Cherry Gardens, and who spoke with a faux Californian accent? Such a story might reflect her life, but handled by a mediocre writer there is no reason to suppose it would be any better than the national literature she had already grown to dislike. She went on to explain that instead she liked reading young adult fantasy and science fiction from America. Clearly she wasn't looking for representation. I suspect like most of us, she just wanted a damn good story. We relate to strong characters not because they share our specific biographies, but because they are convincingly written.

I felt for this girl. What she had said wasn't posturing of any kind. She was being honest to what and how she felt. Yet, the terms she had chosen seemed wrong. Her disappointment, I think, was not in Caribbean literature, but in the examples of it she had encountered during school, books sterile enough to win the approval of the Ministry of Education, books so often plain and lacking in tension that they turn our students away from Caribbean literature rather than kindling their interest in it. I suspect her disappointment was in being forced to read yet another book by C. Everald Palmer (God rest his soul) or by Vic Reid (my father's godfather, so a man for whom I have a soft spot), men who should most certainly be lauded, but who were so invested in writing appropriate national literature for school children, that their output lacked verve, that ability to evangelise and make converts out of their readers. Her disappointment was in an unimaginative and sometimes stale syllabus and in mediocre writers telling mediocre stories.

I tried to tell this student about the amazing Caribbean novels she was not allowing herself to read. Some of the best Caribbean novels

– some in the canon like Erna Brodber's *Myal* and Earl Lovelace's *The Wine of Astonishment*, and newer books such as Shani Mootoo's *Valmiki's Daughter* or Kerry Young's *Pao* – take place in small communities where people chew cane or eat mangoes, but where they come face to face with all the problems and complexities of modernity.

Mediocrity certainly does not lie in the setting of a village, or in the use of patois or in the subject matter of slavery. Mediocrity does not lie in saffron or in saris or in the person of Maas Joe or even in an exploration of his superstitions. And in the student's declaration that she was simply over reading another Caribbean novel written in patois, and on the theme of slavery, she had actually forbidden herself from reading one of the single most ambitious and incredible books of Jamaican Literature in recent years – Marlon James' *The Book of Night Women*.

Funnily enough, it was James who recently made dismissive mention of Maas Joe at a keynote presentation at the 2013 Bocas Festival in Trinidad and who therefore gives the present essay its occasion. On the dangers of creating a national literature, James jibed:

> So take one small rural village, two grannies, a church sister named Dorcas, two wayward children named Lurlene, and one Maas Joe (because there must always be a Maas Joe), throw in some rivers, a mountain, and a brush with obeah, and poof, you have a Jamaican novel!

James' own Jamaican novel boasts a full cast of strong mother-figures, generous dabs of obeah, a few insertions of folk songs, and it is all told in dialect. I imagine such a description, accurate though it may be, would not have sold what is a truly remarkable and gripping novel to the young student I encountered and maybe not to Marlon James himself, who becomes collateral damage to his own thesis.

But I am being unfair. Marlon's talk at the Bocas Festival was, in my opinion, on point for the most part. Marlon understands that to build a house is to simultaneously create two locations – an outside and an inside, and so when we create a house for our national literatures we should immediately be conscious of and interrogate not only who we include, but who we exclude. Who is it that waits out at the gate, knocking, only for us to put our heads out the window and

say, "Nothing today!" Who do we shoo away because they neither fit the racial or sexual profile of a national writer because they do not wear the trappings of the folk? Marlon is rightly worried that people might imagine a country consists of only one kind of folk, and that maybe only one kind of writer is allowed to write that story. And what about middle-class stories? Do they not count as part of the national literature in a developing country?

These are useful questions. It is only Marlon's tongue-in-cheek dismissal of Maas Joe that I think goes too far, and that makes me feel compelled to rise to the old man's defence, but also to my own defence – and to the defence of Marlon who perhaps unwittingly attacks himself – and to the defence of any writer who might wish to write about Maas Joe and his village in all the simplicity or complexity that their talent can manage.

The single word which haunts this essay but which I have not yet invoked is "cosmopolitan". Indeed, we have been talking so far about the anxiety of the cosmopolitan. I would argue that both the Caribbean writer who has as his slogan "Maas Joe Got To Go", and also the reader who affects boredom at all that "folked up" foolishness are people in the grips of such an anxiety. I admit that my own credentials as such a cosmopolitan Caribbean man/writer are strong as well.

My life moves between the UK and Jamaica. In the UK, I live in a converted church; the design there is slick, the floors wooden, the art collection forever growing, and the stock of wine forever being emptied and then replenished. And while you will find art and wine in my living space, you will find precious little of my mother's aesthetics – no puffy satin sheets with embroidered hearts or flowers worked into the pattern; no beaded curtains; no porcelain dogs; no lace doilies laid on the backs of the sofas; no Serenity Prayers on plaques; and on the walls no prints of poor country people collecting water by the lone standpipe in the village. I seem to travel a lot as well, having now been to every continent in the world except Antarctica. I have become undeniably cosmopolitan, and yet it is not a flag I always wish to wave.

Let me be crude: as I see it, the cosmopolitan writer and reader from the Caribbean are those of us who have insisted on locating our intelligence and our savvy in a rejection of ourselves and what we perceive as the embarrassing smallness of our cultures. We want to

prove ourselves wider than that. We are those who have become especially suspicious of big fish in small ponds. This is one of our favourite warning mantras. *Do not become a big fish in a small pond!*, we warn each other. It means that we accept as a given that the large pond of the world is necessarily a better place to swim and live in, than the small, local pond of the Caribbean – and that what is endorsed by the world is naturally and always superior to what is only endorsed by the local. We wish to produce something that is "world-class". We use this phrase "world-class" without pondering what it means to submit so willingly to a new kind of classism, or even reflecting on whose taste it is by whom we are being arbitrated. We are sophisticated, *au fait* with world trends.

But inasmuch as this new cosmopolitan constitutes a new elite, it is a masterful reinvention of former systems of exclusivity and exclusion. What was once white (and ergo, superior), what was once British (and ergo superior), what was once first world (and ergo, superior), has now become cosmopolitan, and ergo superior.

And so it is we have come full circle – in danger of standing against everything we once stood for. With writers such as Junot Diaz, Edwidge Danticat, V.S. Naipaul and Derek Walcott, it is no longer easy for us to claim the periphery. We are not all in the centre but it is obvious that we have access to it in a way we never had before. To get to the centre it might seem one has to be cosmopolitan, and here is where the anxiety flares up. We declare war against Maas Joe and his culture, dismissing the man and his community as not worthy of ambitious literature. In so doing, we impoverish not only ourselves, but the very cosmopolitanism that we are newly committed to. For isn't it glaringly apparent that our contribution to the great muckle is our little mickle; that our contribution to the international is that we are nationals; and our contribution to the cosmopolitan is precisely our ability to traffic in things from those peripheries we happen to have access to. We are the ones able to pull Maas Joe's donkey, braying and all, into the very centre of things knowing the man himself will follow soon. So why do we now wish to leave them in their little field in Effort, Clarendon, simple, guileless, unwritten.

End Notes

1. David Dabydeen, "Nigger Talk in England Today", in *State of the Language*, Ed. Christopher Ricks and Leonard Michaels (London: Faber, 1990), pp. 12-13.

THESE ISLANDS OF LOVE AND HATE
(2008)

Originally published in the *Glasgow Herald*. Commissioned as a response
to the then recent murders of two tourists in the Caribbean.

If you go on vacation to Jamaica, it is not likely you will get to
see or experience it. Around the beachfront property in which
you are staying, there will be a high fence. Like all fences, it keeps
things out. Mainly, it keeps the Caribbean out. The problem is,
you will not see the fence. The landscape artist did his job well
– he managed to give the whole resort an illusion of openness –
the beach on one side bordered only by the horizon, the perfectly
manicured lawns on the other, opening out onto island life behind
it, verdant mountains rising in the distance. The fence is invisible.
Of course there have been tourists – you may have been one of
them – who naturally perceived it, who felt for its weaknesses
and with a deep breath, escaped into the beautifully ugly, the violently
magical, the tragically wonderful thing that is the Caribbean, the
place where I grew up. But that story, of tourists who escape finally
into their true destinations, discovering then that paradise is at
once uglier and more amazing than any brochure could have had
them imagine, is not often told. It is not often told because it is
neither a good nor a bad story. It simply is.

Its opposite, however, is almost always a bad story, and one that is
increasingly told. For there are moments when it is the Caribbean on
the other side that places its large, dark hands against the fence, and
feels for weaknesses. Sometimes it isn't tourists that break out, but
the Caribbean that breaks in. How many times have we bowed our
heads upon hearing this story – Catherine and Benjamin Mullany
who visited Antigua for their honeymoon last year, Claudia Von Weis
who went to Cuba, Melanie Rose Clarke who came to Jamaica for a

wedding, people who found themselves suddenly in the actual place they had flown to – saw it, experienced it, and died for it. In a way, their story isn't new, for hundreds of years people have been discovering the islands of the Caribbean and falling in and out of love with them.

I grew up in Jamaica. But if you ask me what it was like growing up on an island, I would tell you – it never felt like an island. It felt like a country, which is what it was. It felt like the world, which is what it was. None of us live in the whole world at any one time. We live in small portions of it, and we get to know that small portion. I would say, however, that a hotel in the Caribbean *is* like an island – because it is a small place cut off from the world around it. Who can blame the hotels for doing what they do and for being what they are – fenced off, cut off, sterile enclaves, that offer Caribbean culture to their guests in the same way that they offer Caribbean rum – diluted, safe, with pineapples and a cute umbrella? Full-proof Caribbean culture can be dangerous, so for the evening's entertainment the tourist is only given a band of toothless men playing banjos and, throughout the day, smiling women in floral skirts serving mangoes and plantain chips. The tourist watching this parade of pleasant, smiling minstrels will inevitably comment on how slow and easy the pace of life is in the Caribbean. They will have little inkling of the struggle that is always underneath those songs plucked out on the banjos. Who can blame the hotels from shielding tourists from reality? This is the thing they wanted to escape from anyway. But hotels are inevitably controlled by big money interests intent on making even more money, and here is the sad truth of things – if tourists feel at least a little terrified of outside, of the real Caribbean, they will keep themselves (and their money) put. It is a careful balancing act this – making tourists feel safe enough to come to the Caribbean, but not so safe as to venture into it.

There is such a large thing to say right now, about tragedies like the ones in Antigua and Jamaica and Cuba, and how in the assurances given by Antigua's Canadian-born Commissioner of Police or Jamaica's British-born Assistant Commissioner of Police (as if to assure the world that the savage natives do not police themselves) and all the promises of beefed up security around the hotels, how an unfortunate kind of tourism is being perpetuated in the Caribbean.

The tourist is encouraged not to ever really know or to be suspicious of his host. But that thing is truly large and I do not know how to say it exactly. It would have to be a nuanced thing; it would have to make several allowances. After all, big hotels did not create the outside world they seek to protect tourists from: they only exploit it.

Besides, there is an even larger thing to say about the outside world that comes in occasionally – about the Caribbean. It is this world that, for brief moments, whenever there is a tragedy, many will try to understand. It is this world that will be explained through history and sociology, that will be summarized by statistics, GDP, indices of poverty, unemployment rates, homicide rates. But the scientific language of statistics and the language of sociology does not offer a template nor a vocabulary to talk about this larger thing that I want to talk about – about love and hate, and how these things have been brewing in Jamaica, if not the whole Caribbean.

I was born in Kingston. I was born in the time when the word was "love". It was the time of White Flight. It was the '70s. In those days, Jamaica's most charismatic Prime Minister, Michael Manley, mounted a stage and said four words which would become a mantra for the poor. "The word is love," he said. The word is love.

To repeat it now makes it sound like a strange, nebulous thing, a thing without any real substance or meaning. And that was its exact danger. It was a powerful thing that had no meaning. It was like an Old Testament prophecy – it took root in the hearts of the disenfranchised, and they believed that this word would change them and their situations. But it was only rhetoric. In essence, they were empowered into nothing. The strange irony is that the time when the word was love was actually a quite hateful time.

Many, of course, do not and cannot see it this way. After all, so many good things happened. Poor black people who had been previously denied so many good things, who had believed whole-heartedly in their wretchedness and in their physical ugliness, finally began to believe something bigger. To this day there are those who count the decade of the '70s as a success, and maybe in a certain way it was. Many Jamaicans found out suddenly that they could love themselves and who they were – the image they saw in the mirror. They could also look forward to their own possibilities, the things they could suddenly achieve. The big problem was that the govern-

ment had given them all this hope, all this love, this wide sense of possibility, but little way of achieving it.

Jamaicans have always been inventive. Many decided they would achieve their possibilities for themselves. What helped was that at this very moment, the large-scale importation of illegal guns had begun. Take note of the following recipe: arm people with a message and then with a machine gun, and they will believe that the second thing can achieve the first; they will believe that guns can achieve love.

You cannot fault people for trying. They tried and they are still trying now. Of course, it doesn't work. And neither sociology nor homicide statistics can pinpoint the moment when the prophesied love turned into hate. As much as people began to love themselves, was as much as they began to hate everything that had oppressed them before, every system that had kept them down – the police, the upper-class, the middle-class, the government, businesses, the school system, the English language. You see, in that hateful time when I was born, the time when the word was love, all over the island a resentful people began to commandeer vehicles and houses and parcels of land. They drew frightened owners from out of their homes and cars and farms, dumped them onto the streets, and the captors would say triumphantly, "The word is love."

In the time when the word was love, many left. Largely, they were white and Chinese Jamaicans who no longer felt safe. They took their capital with them, leaving Jamaica in an even sorrier state than it was before. Some of these class-war refugees settled in the lands of their summer vacations: Canada, America, England, even Wales like Jeanetta did. Jeanetta became a kind of mother to me when I first moved to Britain. Staying at her home one Christmas, I asked her why she had left Jamaica. I was too young to remember the '70s as I had only lived in that decade for its last year. So she told me, "I was just tired of saying I was sorry. I didn't know how to say it anymore. The island I loved turned around and hated me. They hated me for being white." That same evening in Wales, a neighbour came over and looked at my dark skin and smiled. She declared, "Oh Jeanetta, finally! A proper Jamaican!" I know this statement made her sad, and I realized that this thing which happened in the '70s – when the majority of Jamaicans began to love themselves and began to hate others – is a complex thing with many truths to it, and many

repercussions, and a tragic history projecting itself into the future. I used to imagine Jeanetta back in Jamaica, and I would imagine her in the safe island of a hotel – fenced off from the Caribbean she grew up in and still loves, hoping that it would not break in on her. I only stopped imagining such a thing recently, because Jeanetta really has gone back. She lived in Wales for twenty years, but it is the Caribbean she has always loved.

I have switched places with Jeanetta, and sometimes from this new country, I look back to Jamaica and it is hard for me to understand my own deep love for the place, a country that is occasionally full of such indefensible hatred. And yet, there is something special that grows out of it all – this mix of paradisiacal beauty and poverty, of passion and politics. I understand what it means to be an artist in the midst of all of that – to be a prophet in the midst of Babylon. I understand the power of Peter Tosh who wrote "Get up, Stand up" or Buju Banton who came from Salt Lane, or Bounty Killer who grew up "as sufferer but naah mek him children grow up tun sufferer". Or of Bob Marley flashing his locks and singing over and over, "One love, One heart!" And maybe it is this song, playing in the background of so many "Come to the Caribbean" commercials that convinces potential tourists that the Caribbean Sea really is full of love. And it is. These islands are full of so much love. But sometimes that love goes so deep, it arrives on the other side as its opposite.

A KIND OF SILENCE
(2005)

There is a kind of man born on a Wednesday – the most unremarkable day of the week because it is in the middle of everything, the fulcrum in which no one is really concerned. Sergeant MacDonald was a man who was born on a Wednesday and, worse, he was born in the middle of the day.

It is better to be born in the dawn. A hospital then is like any other business – silent and empty, as if sickness swells and eases with the rush hours and easy hours that are part of any day. Or it is better to be born in the night when people are not distracted by the noise of their own lives and might possibly care that the world is expanding.

At twelve o'clock the hospital is crowded. A woman is holding onto the railing, pulling her hair and screaming "Lord!" and "No!" Maybe her man has died; maybe she is going to die; maybe she escaped from the mad ward. No one knows or tries to find out. It is twelve o'clock and Wednesday and her screams only drown out others which would rise up if she was to quit. And who in all this extravagant, painful fiasco can find the space to give a damn about another woman who comes in breathing hard, her back breaking under the weight of pregnancy?

When Sergeant MacDonald was born the midwife did not say, "It's a boy," though it was part of her script. She was silent. He was born midday on a Wednesday. The ward was crowded. There were other babies to deliver. He opened his eyes; he cried. The midwife cut the umbilical cord and moved on. What else to do?

And he would become that kind of man – who cut cords easily and moves on.

There is a kind of boy born in this world in shit. This isn't an exaggeration.

There are places where people live as wild pigs and hungry dogs; this isn't a metaphor. In Riverton City, Jamaica, pigs and dogs wait every day for garbage trucks to come in. And people wait, just as desperately, to scavenge for food and pieces of cardboard and zinc to build flimsy houses.

When the pigs, dogs and people need to shit, they do it right there. The shit becomes one with the garbage; it hardens into ground. Houses are built on shit and children are born in it.

Marlon was a kind of boy like this. Born without a birth certificate or a last name. He knew the taste of sour meat. He knew how to wrestle pigs for food. Knew how to sneak into yards and stone trees. He knew about the system – about schools not being made for boys who are born without last names. He found out too early about Closed Doors because teachers sent him home for smelling bad. They sent him home to no running water and told him to bathe properly this time. They sent him home for speaking too badly. They sent him home for not having books. And then they sent him home for missing school too many days. A boy who is born in shit is destined to put up with a whole lot of shit and, barring a miracle, is dealt shit his whole life.

Watching the other boys from the swamp, Marlon learned about the small money to be earned at traffic lights, the coins dropped into a dirty hand that could add up – enough, some days, for a meal. He watched and learned the skill of silence – down-turned eyes and a careful listlessness that might move a driver to pity. And, at two or three in the morning, Marlon also learned about Open Doors, the back seat of cars, his pants immediately unbuckled, and even then, the skill of silence.

There is a kind of man in this world who is made for one job, and if, before him, that job did not exist, he will invent it. Sergeant MacDonald was made to be a Jamaican policeman because he was born in the middle of the day on a Wednesday.

In school he had been a boy who might suddenly put down his book, walk across the classroom and punch another child so hard that child would fall. And whoever he had hit never complained, because the truth was they had always done something. Whether that morning or a week before, they had teased MacDonald about something,

shoved him jokingly, or even said something about him in private. With MacDonald crime never went unpunished.

After high school he signed up for the Jamaica Constabulary Force. It was a job he was made for. In Jamaica, a lawyer is only part of the law system. A jury is only part. A judge and the constitution are parts. But a Jamaican policeman is the whole law system. Not just officer, but court and judge and bailiff and hangman. He is Law itself.

There is a kind of woman who one day sits very high but on the other day she comes down low. Everyone will comment on it. They will say, "Look on how things is. De higher monkey climb, de greater him fall. Look how she come down low!"

It is the kind of woman who sits around a table in the evening, a silent maid serving her pumpkin soup, of which she drinks only a few sips. The maid returns and brings back a meal of turkey and potatoes, which she only nibbles; the maid finally brings a slice of pudding, which she might taste. This is the way this high-seated woman lives until the day everything collapses. She will longer have a maid. She will walk round with a calabash bowl begging for salt and at every door she knocks on the people think to themselves, "But look how she come down low."

Jennifer was this kind of a woman, who ends up walking with a calabash bowl begging for salt. She was not born rich – but she was born a schemer and a liar. She stole her mother's good china plate and pawned it for new shoes; she stole her mother's diamond ring for money to go to a party; she stole her mother's money so many times that when she turned eighteen her mother threw her out of the house, cried only once and then forgot she ever had a daughter.

Out in the great wide world she could only survive by scheming. She considered those stories she would hear on radio now and then – an uninsured boy or girl who had a life-threatening disease and couldn't afford the plane fare or the surgery costs for the operation that had to be done in Miami. Appeals would be made for people to put money into such and such an account. A worthy cause.

Jennifer was the monkey who climbed high. When she called the radio programme she almost believed that she really did have a nine-year-old son with a tumour in his brain, who wouldn't reach his tenth birthday if something wasn't done now. She cried and she moved the

radio's heart. A bank account was set up. Appeals were made. It was a two million dollar operation her son needed – and though two million Jamaican dollars is nothing, it still was a figure far beyond poor people's ability.

Two companies gave the full amount anonymously. People gave little and large portions – whatever they could afford. At the bank, Jennifer would check the ever growing figure and pick up little notes that said, "We are praying for you", or "May your child live to see ten."

But maybe every blessing received under false pretence ends up being a curse.

Jennifer had money, but it didn't last forever. She planted herself in a big apartment – with a maid who brought soup, turkey and pudding. Then Jennifer brought in a boyfriend who brought in all the heartache. He was also a liar and a schemer, and he ran off with her money – didn't even know she was pregnant.

So low. She came down low.

When she gave birth to Marlon she was living in Riverton City. His name was not recorded on any birth certificate. And she did not know the principle that the sins of the mother are visited on the child. From the beginning he was cursed, like the fictitious son before him, to die before the age of ten.

There is a kind of night in Jamaica full of its own violence – a kind of night where driving through a ghetto you are likely to see a man running through the street with the handle of a knife protruding from his chest, blood soaking his white T-shirt. Flagging down your car, he is screaming, "Lawd, she stab mi! The bitch stab mi!"

It is the kind of night where you only feel secure when you are in your own bed, surrounded by concrete walls. The concrete walls aren't real security but it gives a feeling that between you and the violence is a barrier. The feeling of security is more important than the fact of it.

But boys from the swamp cannot run from such a night. They live for it. At two or three in the morning, they approach cars that stop by the traffic light, though at two in the morning cars do not need to stop. The boys do not know what will happen and every approach is a gamble – if there was something to lose. But what is there to lose?

Pride – when the driver looks straight ahead and pretends a boy is not leaning against his window, arm outstretched for a dollar? What is there to lose – the purity of young bodies? – when an old man drives up and smiles this smile that has no warmth or comfort in it, who reaches opens the back door saying, "Come in, you're beautiful." What is there to lose? Whatever can be lost has already been lost inside every night that was like this one.

The kind of night in Jamaica that is full of its own violence is in fact every night. So it is hard to tell you what exact date it was that Marlon approached the unmarked police vehicle. It was a night like every other night. The most I can tell you is this: Marlon was nine years old. His tenth birthday had not yet arrived.

After fifteen years in the police force, Sergeant MacDonald built a name for himself and had stories which trailed behind him wherever he went. He was that kind of a police. One story went like this. In the weeks when a vicious gang had held Kingston by the throat, businesses had to be locked down and everyone was scared of downtown. Every day this gang killed someone, twenty-two persons in all, and included in that list were two policemen and a soldier. The Prime Minister called a state of emergency and churches began to pray. Sociologists at the University said it was high time to sit down and think of a long term plan to curb the island's culture of violence.

Sergeant MacDonald, who had been silent during all of this, and who took his authority from no one, one day armed himself with a gun and in that gun was only one bullet. He went downtown to the lane this gang frequented. They were all there, lined up against a wall, armed. MacDonald walked through the confused group of men, straight to the leader of the gang, took out his gun and killed him. He turned to the other men and said, "Time to settle down." For almost a year after that there was a ceasefire in downtown Kingston.

So MacDonald was the kind of officer who was given his own space and his own authority to do his job any way he saw fit. When Marlon, without a last name, approached his unmarked police car that early morning, the sergeant looked on the boy and saw the complete hopelessness of that life. If he was another kind of man, this panoramic view of the boy's life might have become compassion. But

MacDonald was the kind who cuts cords and moves on easily. And he was the law itself, enforcer, court, judge, bailiff and hangman. When he saw this life doomed to hopelessness, and maybe later on to crime, he did not see the sense of it continuing.

A boy who approaches a car window – what does he have to lose? His life; his future; the possible miracle that could have come to turn everything around? Marlon extended his arm; MacDonald took out his gun, pointed it to the boy's forehead and pulled the trigger.

There is a kind of silence in this country that follows the gunshot. A silence in which those in their beds, surrounded by concrete walls, stir slightly. The concrete walls muffle the sound of the gunshot, and give it the illusion of distance. The person in bed whispers a prayer and then goes back to sleep. It is a silence like a matchstick flame, never lasting more than a moment.

There is a kind of surprise which spreads over a little boy's face who has just been shot. It is not a deep surprise. It cannot be. In the split second in which he is shot, the boy does not have time to understand what is happening. And if he does have the time, he does not have a wide enough sense of how things should be, a sense of his possibilities, to feel how wrong this thing is. And Marlon did not have enough life to flash before his eyes – that kind of "enough life" that is always expanding into so much more life, so that in the face of it all ending he can shout, "No! This is not supposed to happen!" Marlon died with a shallow surprise in his eyes.

On this island, there are policemen who have the right to decide who should live and for how long, who should die and when. They have this right, because no one has challenged it. Because we have been silent. Through the island's terrible history of police killings, you will find old men who were on their way home to their grandchildren, little girls who died clutching Barbie-dolls in their hands, unarmed pickpockets shot in the back, the mentally-insane.

There is another person who dies, another kind of person altogether, and for them there is observed a moment of silence. In that moment there is respect and a measure of mourning, a measure of rage and a measure of looking at how the world thins. And maybe that kind of silence is not silence at all.

But to a person like Janice Allen, Cleve Wright, Basil Brown, Otis Simms, Amanie Wedderburn, Yvette Locke, Oneil Martland, Glassmore Gordon, Nicoy Davis, Marlon, Marlon-without-a-last-name, there is for these the kind of silence that is truly silence. The silence of doors shut. Of eyes closed. Of lips sealed. The silence of poverty and of being smothered. The silence of Heaven. The silence of trees that fall in forests or of men who fall in cities, and whose fallings make no sound because there is no one around to hear them. The silence of justice turning its back. The kind of silence we must twist like wire, and break.

A SMALLER SONG
(for Thomas Glave)
(2007)

Thomas, four years ago Chad died. I did not know him. I did
not mourn him at the time; this is not his eulogy. I found out he
died only years after. I was looking for something else completely
and found this article which was so full of the unsaid. I did not
know Chad and neither did his killers, though they felt they knew
him enough. It says, the newspaper article, that he was a softer
boy than most, with long eyelashes and he wanted to go to Art
School. It says he had been recently orphaned, and so he moved
in with his big brother. But the people from the community said,
"How two man fi live in the same house, eh? Yu nuh know seh
we kill battybwoy?" So they killed him. He had gone outside one
night, because, I imagine, the house was too small and he was
thinking of his large future which would not fit into the living
room; Portmore houses can be so stifling. He went outside to
neighbours who were offended by his softness and by his eyelashes
and by the fact that he lived with his brother who like all brothers
was, unfortunately, male – his big brother who loved him and
who, at the sound of gunshots, would find him minutes later,
his eyes fluttering and looking at nothing, his lips trembling, and
the night full of the awful sound of him gargling on blood. And
I imagine that when the killers walked away, they were singing a
song.

 Today in Jamaica, my friend's mother calls him and her mouth is
sweet with gossip. She speaks of a man on campus who unfortunately
was not killed yesterday. Who unfortunately was saved, though he
did not deserve salvation; though his life had been forfeit; though the
mob of angry students made rightful demands of his heart and all of
his insides, which in fact, was not his but theirs; though the crowd

reminded the guards into whose small room the man run, that people like him should dead. And on the phone today, my friend's mother agrees, people like him should dead. She agrees, unknowingly, that her son should be dead.

I imagine his small body slaughtered, and his mother singing gloriously, singing happily, over it. She is singing the same song Chad's killers sang. And Thomas, the song you sing is its opposite and its antidote. It is the song that should have been in the mother's mouth instead. Your song, Thomas, is brave; it is big; it is right. Someone must sing it; many people must sing it, with feeling, with whooping and with adlibs.

It's just that somewhere along the way I misplaced all the things that had to do with God, though I never wanted to, and now I end up mistrusting all gospels, all pulpits and all messages – even my own. And this business of speaking from the podium of dead bodies, and gaining leverage from the crucified, makes me uncomfortable. I know the fight we must fight. I am fighting it too, although some days I think guiltily, it is more glorious to fight for freedom than to have it. But I know the song you are singing; most days I sing it with you. It is an old maroon song that starts with the sound of an abeng. It is accompanied by the fife and by drums. It is a freedom song for the people below the surface trying to emerge. It is a big and a terrible song. But forgive me, Thomas, if right now, I choose to sing a smaller one. Sometimes your song is bigger than my mouth. You must continue to sing it all the same, because you sing for Chad, and you sing for all the men who were unfortunately saved, and all the men who even more unfortunately weren't. You sing a song for me. And you sing a song for Brian.

It is now two years since he died. I am not convinced that his was a hate crime. But he was hated, and now he is dead, and perhaps that is all we need to know. But when your song rose over his body, the same song full of mourning, a song full of what was lost, we could not then sing for what he had gained. It was as if, Thomas, your voice, which is always breaking the terrible silence, had suddenly imposed another one. And we had to pretend we were eternally defeated people. We had to pretend we were not maroons after all. We had to write to Amnesty like shackled people waiting on Queen Victoria to set us free. We had to pretend no battles had been won, when some

had. And maybe, maybe they were not the big battles. No treaty has been signed. But we have won small things. And on days when the terribleness is too big, and your song is too big, and the sadness comes upon me like wings, and I think I will fly away from this island, then I try to remember the smaller things. I try to sing a smaller song.

I sing a smaller song for the magical ways we exist underground. You might point out that to live *under* is not to live. It is the same as death and as coffins. You might pray *Everyday above ground is a good day*. There is truth in this. But I've always felt giddy about the menacing secret of our society. I've felt that more spirit is under the earth than over it, and there is power in the way we move as poltergeists, like bodiless things that could possess you if you were found walking one night without a crucifix. And I sing for that.

I sing a smaller song because we gather. Because as awful as this country can be, I have known men from Grenada, and men from Dominica and men from Barbados, who come here because they find their own islands too lonely. I sing for those secret houses in Stony Hill, and Jacks Hill, and yes – the back verandah of Brian's house. I sing because of the music we always turn on its head. Boom bye to who when we still here. I sing because we gather, and we dance.

I sing a smaller song for the ways spoat can real out – eeeeeeyyy! The way we talk our talk. The way we speak loudly, but only the right people hear us. I sing for that secret language, lyrical and as coded as drums. There is also a language that is no secret at all. A small song for that too – for the social column I read ten years ago and found the writer addressing his readers as "dovecakes" and "daaaahlings". He is still writing today – in Jamaica – every week his voice is printed, and I wonder if things are as silent as you or I make them out to be.

I sing a smaller song for the ways we exist flamboyantly and invisibly at the same time. Yes, I've gone back to the magical ways of being. The ways we exist incredibly. Haven't you seen us in New Kingston? In gold shirts and in pocketless pants. The bold transgression of our hips. The absolute fierceness of our lisps. And despite it all, we dodge the radars. Isn't that incredible, Thomas? Some days, isn't it something to sing about?

BUT IN GLASGOW, THERE ARE PLANTAINS
(2008)

A little more than twenty-nine years ago I was born in Jamaica. Barring a three month fellowship spent last year at the University of Iowa, and twelve months of postgraduate work in England in 2005, the Caribbean had been my home – the place where my mail was delivered – the place where all sounds had and continue to make immediate sense. It is the place where I never calibrate my accent to make it understood. For those twenty-nine years, I lived in Hope Pastures, a suburb on the outskirts of Kingston. I lived with my parents. I have found that this can be a slightly curious fact to people who live in more developed countries, that at my age I had not yet moved out. It didn't seem so curious to me in Jamaica where the economy doesn't readily give freedom and keys and concrete and windows to young people. But while the exact age for the possibility of flight from nests might differ from culture to culture, its inevitability is consistent, and so as I approach thirty, an urgency has indeed been growing to leave (not necessarily Jamaica), just to create a home that was my own. The big problem was this: I was a writer; I had decided that anything I did had to be connected to writing in some way. In other words, I had decided to be poor.

Three years ago my books up and left me. They had also been in search of their own homes and had little success finding one in the Caribbean, though they had tried. Finally, without the need to pay huge fees or join long queues to get the required visa, they moved, one by one, from a computer where they were composed in Hope Pastures, to the United Kingdom. My first poetry collection went to Heaventree Press in Coventry, my short stories went to Macmillan in Oxford, my second poetry collection moved up north to Manchester where Carcanet gave it shelter, and my novel made its home in

London with Weidenfeld & Nicolson. Perhaps it was always inevitable that I would follow my works across the ocean, to be closer to them, and so six months ago, I moved here, to Scotland, to Glasgow.

I map out that timeline to make the simple point that this is all new to me. I know that in me and my biography there is now an undeniable Scottish-Caribbean connection. I know that I'm looking at Glasgow and understanding it through Caribbean eyes, but I'm not sure the few observations I've made in six months can come with any real depth or profundity. This is necessarily an essay of first impressions.

As my departure approached, my friends became excited that I was moving to Glasgow. When news of the attempted bombing at the airport exploded onto international news, they all called, not so much concerned as impressed that I was moving to a city important enough to be the target of terrorists. It seemed to them that Glasgow, and they apologized for not having known it before, was right up there with New York and London, a bustling metropolis, a centre of all things new, forward and diverse. Even my excitement grew, I must admit. Even now, when anyone in the UK finds out that I'm living in Glasgow, they say "Wow – that's a city with quite a buzz about it, isn't it?"

I'm not sure how to answer that very leading question any more – how to say, yes and no. You see, I realize I've gotten into the habit of demanding of big and growing cities that they be multi-everything. Multicultural, multilingual. That they be diverse in economy and the peoples that populate it. Almost, it seems to me now, they be everything but themselves. Perhaps we feel rightly that variety is a sign of health and a multiplicity of ideas. And Glasgow *is* diverse. The staunch testimonies of people who have lived here for many more years and decades than my own paltry six months will attest to that. There are Indian restaurants, Asian supermarkets and African communities. In 1999, Glasgow became the UK's first official Dispersal City, helping to take some of the overflow of refugees and asylum seekers that had been crowding London. So from Vietnamese Boat people, to Bosnians, to Iraqis, Scotland as a whole and Glasgow in particular is more diverse than it has ever been.

"Wow, you live in Glasgow," the people say, "that's a city with quite the buzz about it, isn't it?"

Yes, is all I say now, but to myself I think further thoughts. I think Glasgow is not like New York or London where I know I can always find a place, because in New York and London there are several worlds, a few of which I can belong to. In Glasgow, there is only Glasgow. It is a city which will never stop being itself. You must learn to fit into that city – which doesn't mean you're not welcome. I've had to think what it means when I've called back home and said to my inquiring friends, that Glasgow is great, it's fantastic, it's just that it's not exactly the most diverse city in the world. And I realize that I am not really looking or listening out for diversity – I am actually looking and listening out for myself. In the swell of immigrants and languages, I do not hear sounds that make immediate sense to my own ear. On some days, in the city centre, on Buchanan Street, a black man strums a guitar, and sings Bob Marley songs so convincingly you sometimes, for just a second, think it might be a CD playing. But then in those spaces where his voices reveals, not the singer he has adored and mimicked his whole life, but himself, I realize he isn't from my part of the world at all.

You must not laugh, but my first impression of Glasgow was of a place that was full of the sun. I had come for an interview at the University and the day was uncharacteristically warm. Students were lounged out in the grass, many of them shirtless, throwing Frisbees and eating ice cream. As the man who would eventually become my line manager walked me across the lawn, he tried to sell the university to me and said, pointing at the sun and the people basking in it – "Look Kei, this is what Heaven will be like."

I looked and then I frowned. "So it's true then, sir," I mumbled, "there really are no black people in heaven."

For the first time in my life, I am I living in a place of my own choosing, paying my own rent, buying my own furniture, making my own home. As a man from the Caribbean, but living in Glasgow, you must say a kind of mantra to survive. Mine goes like this:

In Glasgow my flat is red and orange and green; people who enter say, with delight, what bright Caribbean colours! They are Ikea colours – but it's true, I have been trying to make the place warm with more than just the heat from Scottish Gas. I've been trying to conjure up an island in that tiny flat. I also have orange and green bamboo

sticks stuck behind the couch, not because they fit into the colour
scheme, or because this is an aesthetically pleasing choice but because
(and my mother would be confused by it – her eyes falling glumly
onto the protruding sticks, she'd say, "What the hell is that!?") this
kind of foreignness makes the space my own. For every immigrant
there is a complex interaction and negotiation between notions of
local and foreign. But while we might try to infuse our new homes
with a sense of what is beautiful that was developed somewhere else
far away, there are also parts of ourselves – the ways in which we were
always *other*, in that other place – that can now find the space to
flourish. It is our own "foreignness", a foreignness that was always
local to our hearts, that is now growing. I'm perhaps just warning
myself to be careful of these categories of foreign and local, Scottish
and the Caribbean, when it is the nature of the individual in his
travels, whether actual or virtual, whether across the world or across
the road, to see things, borrow, reject and revise himself and his
tastes. What is happening to me in Scotland, as I establish a home, is
what is happening to everyone in this world everyday – we are still
and always becoming ourselves.

In Glasgow you can be sure to see fat women on the streets in small
shirts, the equators of their stomachs displayed proudly and they look
on you with an attitude that says, "What? What?" and I smile because
I think I've known these women my whole life, and I'm happy I did
not leave them behind in the Caribbean. In Glasgow, while you are
certain to see the girth of women, you cannot always see the skies,
or perhaps I should say, you cannot always see the sky's blueness.
What a miracle it is when that happens. You appreciate it all the
more because of how carefully blue is rationed. Whenever they hear
my accent in Glasgow, the taxi men tell me what must be a shared
joke in this country. They say, *Son, if you don't like the weather, just wait
five minutes.* In Glasgow, you cannot always see the mountains – but
they are there; the highlands rise magnificently to the north of the
city, and they remind me of the Caribbean I've known. The popular
Haitian proverb goes, "Behind the mountains are more moun-
tains", which speaks, of course, to the never-ending of trials some
people have had to go through for generations, but is also a simple
description of the landscape of the Greater Antilles – mountain
after mountain after mountain – a fact which has made so many

Caribbean people feel exposed and afraid in flat landscapes uninter-
rupted by mountains.

Far, far south of Glasgow is a big city called London. There, I do
not stop people on the street to ask for directions. I did once, and it
made me depressed. I was depressed by how people held their heads
straight, and how they pretended not to hear me, deciding I was some
kind of street beggar. To the north of London is another city called
Manchester where I lived for a year and fell deeply in love with the
place, because at a small moment of confusion at a traffic light, lifting
my head to search for a road sign to remind myself which street I was
on, two old white women reached up and touched my hands and
asked "Are you alright, luv?" And the fact that they called me love, me,
a black man who they'd never met, means that I will always hold that
city in my heart. Glasgow, however, managed to top even that.
Probably it was the alcohol and the sense of conviviality that New
Year's Day, Hogmanay, brings to Scottish people, but that was my
first day in Glasgow, and walking from Byers Road back to Kelvin
Bridge where my flat was, I have never been hugged by so many
strangers in my life – and I do not care that they were all drunk, I have
decided to accept every hug freely given on that night as an "Aye,
welcome, we're happy to have you here."

In Glasgow, I am learning how to cook the Caribbean. It is not
really that some sudden wave of homesickness has come over me, or
that I never cooked before. I've always loved cooking, but in the
Caribbean I had never tried to cook mackerel rundown, or gungo
peas soup, or escoveitch fish, partly because so many people could do
it better than I could ever even attempt. In Scotland, the Caribbean
becomes a cuisine that I can master – and as I said before, it is often
the case that we can become our home-selves most in places away
from that home – like my middle-class Jamaican friends who, having
migrated to places in the United States like Ohio, found the sudden
ability to speak a Caribbean dialect they had never dared speak in their
very proper houses – or even like the man I met in Toronto, who had
lived there for over twenty years, who dismissed the possibility of
ever going back to Jamaica. "Me," he said, "Mi naah guh back deh?
No sah! Mi naah tell nuh lie. Mi hate Jamaica, Mi bitter it. Me'd a
nevah guh back!" Impossible, I thought, you've already taken the
island with you.

So it is, in my current cooking and the smells that come from my kitchen, I am self-identifying with the Caribbean – but also, it must be said, with Scotland. You see, it is not enough to learn how to make red peas soup – if you are good, you must make it your own, with your own special touch. I am learning to cook the Caribbean with Scottish ingredients, and dare I say I'm becoming good at it. I think I now prefer my Johnny cakes to anything served at that house in Hope Pastures – something about the self-rising flour from Lidl, the sprinkle of fine cornmeal from the delicatessen on Great Western Road; all these combine to make a fried dumpling so much softer and lighter and sweeter than the version my mother made. When I tell my mother the things I've been making, she says that I am becoming stoosh – because sometimes I can't find the exact things I need so I make do. My first attempt at escoveitch fish, I couldn't find the tiny sprats that we usually deep-fry, so I confessed to my mother that I had discovered instead, escoveitch salmon. I told her that curried lamb tastes every bit as good as curried goat – and without the hassle of bones. I have found that my plantain tarts baked in a kind of muffin cup, with Amoretto liqueur mixed into the filling and shredded coconut covering the top tastes better than any plantain tart I have had back home. And when I tell my mother this, she asks, "Are there really plantains in Glasgow?"

In Glasgow it is cold. In Glasgow it rains a lot. In Glasgow, when I moved, the trees were like skeletons. In Glasgow the sounds have not begun to pour gently in my ears, rather, they bang hard against the side of my head. But in Glasgow, mother, there are plantains. And it is these simple things. Plantains more consistently than you find them in Jamaica – as if they import them from a place untouched by hurricanes. In Glasgow, I buy plantains from a little shop on Great Western Road called Solly's, and there you can also find scotch bonnet peppers, which I'd never reflected on before – these peppers I've always thought of as Jamaican peppers, but which had obviously reminded someone, a long time ago, about something he saw in Scotland – a Tam o' Shanter hat, apparently. These connections go both ways! Mother, at Solly's you can buy fresh goat meat, and packets of Maggie soup; you can get tinned callaloo and tinned ackee, and the fact of these

items, these traces of the Caribbean in Scotland, makes me confident there must be others of us here – in Scotland, in Glasgow, even in the West End. I haven't met them yet. Solly's seems to cater to a mainly African clientele. But one day I will go there and linger for a long while; I will stand all day by the shelf where the tinned ackees are kept, and finally when a young woman or man comes in and reaches for a tin, asking the proprietor, "Uncle, how much yu selling de ackee dem for?", I will then introduce myself, one immigrant from the Caribbean to another, "Hey, how you been finding it here?"

IMAGINING NATIONS
(2008)

It was a curious fact I knew growing up, that having been on a plane, and having landed, it is customary that Jamaicans clap, sometimes wildly. In truth, this habit embarrassed those of us who considered ourselves more cosmopolitan – this vigorous applause, this congratulations offered to the pilot and his great skill, this "Thank de Lord that we mek it alive", this stunned appreciation for the magic of it all. A favourite anecdote amongst middle-class Jamaicans, an anecdote which too often was true, involved the first flight of some man or woman, inevitably from the country, who was caught either desperately sucking at their swivel sticks, calling to the air-stewardess with an insistent cry of – *Waitress! Waitress!* or else leaning over to tell us that most famous euphemism, how they *forgot their reading glasses* and so could we help in filling out their customs or immigration forms. So this habit of clapping seemed to belong, almost entirely, to that class of country bumpkins, while I, sadly, was from that class of Jamaicans who mocked it.

There is not much to mock anymore. It seemed to be only a memory of my childhood. On flights to and from the United States, it hardly ever happens. On flights to England it has become rare. However, on flights from England to Jamaica, the habit lives on, and this has finally made me understand something about the gesture which I hadn't been able to read in all my years growing up, my condescension having hidden it from me.

Flights between Jamaica and the United States are, of course, very common now, coming in and going out to many different cities at many different times during the day. Because of the competition between carriers, they aren't always a huge financial burden and they aren't terribly long; at least between Florida and Kingston a flight can

be just an hour and a half. Many Jamaicans who have the means "pop over to Miami" on the weekend to shop. Despite stricter and stricter immigration policies, and despite a forever-long queue of hopeful (yet eventually disappointed) people standing, sweating and fanning themselves desperately outside Kingston's US embassy, the connections between the United States and Jamaica are multiple and profound. My suggestion then is that travel between the US and Jamaica has become so common, so ubiquitous that it has long lost its magic; people have stopped being impressed, they have stopped clapping.

On the flight from Jamaica to England, there is something different happening that mutes the applause. I think this has to do with a journey that starts in the evening in Jamaica, that flies the long haul through the night and then finally comes into the grey sunrise of London. The weary traveller, waking up and realizing that cold and the hustle of commute on the tube awaits him, can barely manage to congratulate the pilot for taking him back to this reality.

But then there is the flight from London to Jamaica.

The first time I took such a flight was in 2005. I had been in England for six months, a poor student, writing my novel in a small room that was actually part of the house where Charlotte Bronte penned *Jane Eyre* – or so the plaque outside the building said. I didn't care for this coincidence. *Jane Eyre* had never been a favourite text. Though my time in England had been a relatively short one, it was still the longest I had lived away from the island, where I had left family, friends and love of course. So this trip back home, which no one in fact knew about, filled me with all kinds of excitement – the excitement of homecoming, of surprise, of warmth. I wasn't long in Gatwick airport before I realized that everyone en route to Jamaica was similarly thrilled. Friendships were formed quickly, people talked to each other in the various queues and in the waiting lounge as if they had known each other from way back when. The conversations, which went in and out of British and West Indian accents, were lively and included the exchange of recipes, the swapping of photographs, and this recurring theme: *Child, I can't tell you when last I see home. It been a long time man! Lawd, I can't even count the years sometimes. Man! It expensive bad fi go home, I had was to save up for this. You know I come over here on a ship, almost fifty years*

*ago. Young man, you never even born dem times, now look on me going
back on a plane, have mercy!*

It is a nine hour journey from London to Kingston and, with each
hour passed, the excitement on that plane grew. After four hours the
old woman beside me shouted angrily, *Jesus son of Mary, I want my
stew peas! Why we can't land now?!* She said she was diabetic and tried
to sleep but could not. She wasn't the only one agitated, longing
desperately to have her feet walk on a land she had left so long ago.
After nine hours, the sky incredibly bright, a blue-green ocean
occasionally showing itself clearly below, boats dotting it, it was as if
the excitement had become too heavy for the plane to carry and it was
the excitement and longing that brought it down onto the island. I
remember the day was blue – a blue so ostentatious that even after a
mere six months I had forgotten that days could look like that. There
was spontaneous, magnificent applause. And what hurts me to this
day is that, sitting on my other side was a young British couple who
immediately began to chuckle at this applause. They chuckled in the
same way I used to as a child – as if to say, look at these parochial
islanders; it made me feel ashamed and I kept my hands to my side.

<div align="center">★</div>

I have begun to wonder how it is the Caribbean immigrant in
Britain survives the distance. The answer is sometimes a sad one:
many of us haven't. The highest incidence of patients suffering
from schizophrenia in the United Kingdom has for many years
been among West Indian migrants. At other times the answer is
a simple one: because we had to. The flight from England to the
Caribbean fetches a steep price, and so frequent connection with
the countries of our birth is economically impossible for most
of us. But beyond the question of affordability, there is a further
hesitation: we are, after all, children of exodus. In some way or
the other, we escaped something and many feel conflicted about
going back to countries whose reputations declined even further
after we left. Our islands are continually presented to us as places
of increasing violence, corruption and backwardness. Furthermore,
we grew up on the bible. We know the story of Lot's wife who
fled, but turned around to look – a simple and automatic gesture
of regret, of goodbye – and for this she was turned into a pillar
of salt. The truth is, many migrants prefer to hold on to a soft,

nostalgic image of their former homes, even if outdated and untrue; they prefer this to going home for a potentially depressing update.

It is easy for the immigrant to hold on to such nostalgic images. Indeed, I would like to suggest that for those who *have* survived the distance – without the luxury of yearly trips back "home" – that their strategy has involved a complicated act of imagination. Despite the simplistic ways the Caribbean has been presented as almost antipodean to England – England is cold, Jamaica is warm, the English are stoic, Jamaicans are wild – Jamaican immigrants have largely succeeded in imagining their own versions of Jamaica onto their British surroundings. This is scarcely remarkable. The strategy of imaging and imposing an old nation-home onto a new landscape has surely always been the habit of the diasporic subject. We need only to look at examples of recent colonialism for evidence of this. In every British city, in almost every West Indian island, in Bombay, in Sydney, and in Toronto, there is bound to be a King Street, a Queen Street, a Princess Street, an Oxford Street, and a Victoria Park somewhere. The indigenous fruit of colonial territories often don't have the dignity of their own names, but are called apples, pears or cherries, not according to their actual genus, but according to their colours, shapes or sizes that might have triggered some yearning memory in the colonist.

The tables have now turned as the Jamaican poet Louise Bennett recognised in her famous poem, "Colonization in Reverse". It is now the previously colonized subject who is confidently imagining his nation onto the colonizer's land. In a world characterized by the breaking down of transnational boundaries, innovations in containerised shipping, and a market-driven economy, what has emerged are niche markets – diasporic communities with culturally specific tastes and longings – and nowadays with money to spend. The process of a Jamaican successfully imagining his island onto London is now an easy one.

I have walked through Brixton and forgotten where I was. But I try to shop there regularly now. The list of products available to me on my most recent excursion is one that makes even my family back home in Jamaica, jealous. This was my shopping list – all of which I managed to get:

- Green bananas (to boil and eat with ox liver of course, or Jamaican callaloo and salted codfish – items I already had stocked in my pantry).
- A breadfruit to roast.
- Banana chips and plantain chips to nibble on.
- Browning sauce – very necessary for the flavour and colour of Jamaican Christmas cake.
- Ginger bulla – a kind of sweet bread.
- Hardough bread.
- Spiced bun – both the loaf, and the round small ones that come packaged in plastic bags.
- Salt mackerel to make mackerel run-down.
- Tinned Jack fruit. (I'm not sure what to do with this yet).
- A bottle of Pure Bulk Syrup (I swear it tastes better than any other).
- Cans of Vienna sausages for breakfast.
- Maggie Cock Soup (the name alone apparently makes it unmarketable to British consumers).
- Gungo peas for either soup, or rice and peas.
- Coarse cornmeal to make either porridge or cornmeal dumplings.

My family in Jamaica are amazed at this bounty, not simply because it seems to them incredible that I should get these products so far away from "home", but because they are all available at the same time. It is much like that play, "Caribbean Nights and Days", which causes poor Ella O'Grady in Erna Brodber's novel, *Myal*, to go clean out of her mind. Ella has a nervous breakdown when her American husband uses the stories of her life in Jamaica as material for a play.

> Ella told her stories well and Selwyn had listened well. The breadfruits looked like breadfruits and the breadfruit trees like breadfruit trees. The star-apples were nice and shiny balls, some purple, some green. You could eat them. The rose-apples were there, tiny and pale yellow and there were some luscious mangoes. But this Grove Town in which Selwyn set his play, had to be the most fruitful place in the whole world and one which respected no seasons. There were breadfruits at the same time as there were star-apples as there were mangoes. Selwyn knew nothing about Easter as star-apple time, mid-summer

for mangoes and the end of summer, the breadfruit season. Nothing at all. It was unnatural.[1]

For better or worse, Brixton has become this image for me, like Selwyn's play, a place which offers, simultaneously, every season (and seasoning) of Jamaica. Now, whatever strain or flavour of nostalgia the immigrant experiences, whatever whim or craving he might have for home, that longing can be satisfied. He does not have to wait on Christmas to have gungo peas, on Easter to have bun and cheese, he need not worry that the passing of a storm will deprive him of sweet plantains for the next three months. He can imagine Jamaica onto his London surroundings whenever he wants.

<p style="text-align:center">★</p>

I was already living here in Glasgow at the time of the 2008 Beijing Olympics. In fact, when the games started I had only recently returned from a trip to Jamaica and I wished desperately to have been in Kingston, watching my small country's success with everyone else, being a part of what became a carnival-like-euphoria, but I couldn't afford to go back again so soon. I had to make do. I bought a TV, though I had sworn against ever getting one, declaring them too distracting and mind-numbing. But alas, what to do? I went out to a nearby second-hand shop and bought one, jogging with it back home in time to catch the opening ceremony. Thereafter I would often be on the phone screaming excitedly with my mother during each race – *Run, Asafa! Run, bwoy!*

Jamaica was the undisputed superstar in the track and field events. Usain Bolt not only won gold in the 100 metres final, but broke the world record while actually slowing his pace for the last ten metres. The women's 100 metres final was incredible for another reason – Jamaica copped the top three places – and it wasn't gold, silver and bronze, but gold, silver and silver – an absolute tie for second. In the women's 200 metres final, Veronica Campbell took the gold, while Usain repeated his world-record-setting, gold-copping ways for the men's 200 metres final. Melanie Walker won the 400 metres hurdles.

During the Olympics an even more complicated process of imagining nations unto other landscapes happened. Back at home in Jamaica, many Jamaicans watched the games communally in Half-

Way-Tree, a commuter thoroughfare in outer Kingston, where large screens had been erected. Because of the time difference, the races were shown in the mornings while many were commuting to work, and so many of these workers would just pause there in the middle of their journeys to watch the games on these screens. Soon many people weren't commuting *through* Half-Way-Tree but commuting to it. Half-Way-Tree became a virtual stadium, and indeed it didn't take long before it was dubbed, "Beijing, Half-Way-Tree". There was hardly a Jamaican who wanted to be in actual Beijing. They wanted to be in their imagination of it. What was happening in this new Half-Way-Tree Bird's Nest Stadium was so phenomenal that international reporters began reporting from there.

In Glasgow, with the TV on in one room, while I worked in another, I had again that Brixton experience of forgetting where I was. I would hear a news report and a woman being interviewed exclaiming – *Lawd Jeezas mi glad mi glad glad mi cyaa even describe it to yu de way mi out fi buss wid joy right now!* And it would seem to me that I was back home in Jamaica, and that the sound in the background was my father watching TVJ news, and not in fact that I was alone in Glasgow listening to the BBC, reporting from Beijing, Half-Way-Tree.

Perhaps it was these news reports that made the Jamaican Diaspora in England realize what they were separated from, what they were missing, this outburst of a complex nationalism which could not be purchased in Brixton Market. So on August 22, 2008, they gathered. Thousands of Jamaicans flocked to Trafalgar Square as if to replace its dwindling population of pigeons. They came out to watch the men's 100 metres relay finals. They came to watch it together. They came to watch it as a nation. The gathering was a explosion of yellow, green and black flags; it was a cacophony of whistles – and what they were doing is this – they were recreating Half-Way-Tree for themselves. While Jamaicans at home imposed Beijing onto Half-Way-Tree, Jamaicans in Britain were imposing Half-Way-Tree onto Trafalgar Square – the very heart of London, that most English of spaces. The conversations in that virtual stadium were the same ones I had heard in the queue and in the waiting lounge at Gatwick Airport – *We haven't been home in so long. Bwoy, I can't even count the years sometimes. Lawd it so expensive to go home I had was to come here today.*

You know, I come over here on a ship, 50 years ago, you never born dem times, now look on me…

The men's team did win that relay finals, and they won it by what seemed to be an actual rather than a metaphoric "clear mile". That is a fact. But what cannot ever be adequately described is what that victory unleashed in Trafalgar Square re-imagined as Half-Way-Tree re-imagined as Beijing. It was as if a plane from England had landed in Jamaica. No. It was as if a thousand such planes had landed. First, of course, there was clapping, then shouting, escalating into screaming, into jumping, into waving and the lifting of hands, into fainting, into hugging, into tears. And then something extraordinary – these thousands of Jamaicans, weeping, began to sing their national anthem. In a most fantastic moment of transnational imagination, they imposed upon Trafalgar Square, the anthem of another country. How strange that was – to look down on the concrete squares of England, and declare to it three times, as if in a spell, as if unlocking a magic that would make their declarations real, would turn the landscape into *Jamaica, Jamaica, Jamaica land we love*.

End Note

1. Erna Brodber, *Myal* (London: New Beacon Books, 1988), p. 83.

WRITING WITH ELEPHANTS
(2010)

I don't think I can live without elephants. When I write there is always one in the room. Not the metaphoric kind – those large obvious things we never get around to saying; and not the 15,000 lb. kind out of Africa or India, but just a small carved one, its trunk lifted, always turned to the window for good luck. My Buddhist friend once assured me of this meaning. She came into my college dorm room and found the elephant in exactly this position, as if bored and looking out onto the streets while I did my work. I didn't believe in it then though I was writing my first novel and needed luck. And I don't believe in it now. But it has become my habit nonetheless, and sometimes I lie and say I cannot live or write without the elephant.

I wanted a ritual. Other writers have theirs. Isabel Allende starts all her novels on January the 8th. My friend, Mike, writes his stories onto the computer with the font-colour turned to white so that he doesn't actually see what he's writing while he's writing it, because that would distract him (it makes me think of spies who would write one letter in ink, and another secret letter on the same page with milk). So I decided on this elephant thing even though I don't believe in it. And nowadays I think I chose it precisely because I don't.

The question of belief is something I find myself returning to in my stories and poems – whether it concerns the quite normal things that we believe in, or the unbelievable things that we believe in, or the unbelievable things that happen to us despite our belief that they won't happen. Some have said that what I write is Magic Realism. I am in two minds about the term. It's probably the best that we can do, but it occurs to me that there are people (like the warner woman who I wrote about in my last novel) who would read the stories I write and say, "But such things happen every day. This is nothing incredible. It

is simple reality." And someone might read this very piece and say, "But of course you must turn an elephant to the window for good luck!" Other people say that I write about people's superstitions. This is a term I definitely do not like, because "superstition" is what we call a belief that we don't share. There is too much condescension in the word.

I grew up in Jamaica. There are no elephants there, not even in the zoo, though our wood carvers still make them. The most popular wooden carvings however, sold in a place called Fern Gully, are of tall Rasta men sporting massive cocks, which stretch out even longer than their impressive heights. Maybe this is an unbelievable thing that some people believe about Jamaican men, and I should write about it that in a future novel. I once thought about buying one of these, but they are too large, and if I put one in my office, turned to the window, it might scare the neighbours.

So I've stuck with elephants. I now have quite a collection and sometimes a friend might give me one as a gift. I give them away, too; I'm not precious about them. And I even have a very tiny white one that can fit in the smallest pocket. I take this one with me on airplanes, and when, mid-flight, I open up my laptop to write, I take the elephant out and allow it to look outside on the passing clouds.

MY MOTHER'S MANY MOUTHS
(2009)

1. The Goat Mouth

About seven years ago my mother had a minor stroke. It was so minor she didn't even know she had had it. What she described to us was a new strangeness in her body. And her mouth sagged a little to one side. She came home one day, in the aftermath of this minor stroke, hitting the door softly and whimpering for someone to let her in; she couldn't manage the effort of taking out her keys, fitting one into the door and then turning it. She was crying when I opened the door, upset that I had taken so long to reach it. She was standing in a puddle of her piss. We took her to the hospital where an MRI scan confirmed the stroke.

A year later my mother fell and her bones broke. It was off to the hospital again where this time they found out that her kidneys were not working properly. This was why her bones were so weak. The kidneys failed soon after and ever since my mother has had to go the hospital twice a week for dialysis treatment. From all these trips to the hospital, all these interactions with people on their way out, my mother has gained a most unsettling talent. She is able to see the inner-clock ticking inside each person, and she can read how much time is left on it. More than once, this goat-mouthed woman (that is how we would say it in Jamaica) has come home from her dialysis treatment to say of Mr So-and-so, "Lawd, I just don't like how he did look today. I give him until Tuesday." And there is no surer death sentence than this.

My Uncle Robert died this morning. I am more than a little sad, and yet I expected it, because when he had just been diagnosed with cancer and there was still the hope of treatment – my mother shook her head dismissively and pronounced, "I don't care what the doctors say... I give him until March."

Like all talented prophets sometimes it seems it is my mother's declarations that make these events happen. Sometimes it seems to me that were she to give Mr So-and-so, or Uncle Robert, until December, or until the next decade even, or until forever, then it would simply have been so. To speak frankly, I am now reluctant to introduce my mother to any friend who might be feeling a little under the weather. I fear she would take no note of their ailment being something simple like the common cold, and she might say to them, "My dear, if you have anything to say to anybody, you best tell them before next-week Wednesday. I give you until then."

2. The Loud Mouth

My sixty-year-old mother is not as strong today as she once was. This is an inevitable fact of aging and of the stroke. But when I was little, I thought that if my parents were to ever get into a physical fight (sometimes it seemed quite close), my mother would have taken out my father in a second. Things are different today; she needs help walking, and she leans on him for support. Her body is smaller too, though for this, she is (as we say it) pleased as Miss Thomas Puss. It is with the utmost insincerity that she complains about her clothes that *just don't fit no more*! Still, as an act of charity, she passes on the oversized garments to women for whom she has reserved a special pity: *Lawd*, she might sigh, *Janice just not doing anything about her weight!*

With her illness it might seem to some people that my mother is diminishing, but they would be wrong. What has not diminished is the decibel and timbre of her voice. My mother has always been a loud woman. I resented this fact growing up. Her voice could find me wherever I was. I might have been outside, for instance, blissfully playing in the yard, and then as if from out of some cloud: *Drew! Drew! Drewww! Dreeeewww! Dreeeewwww!* (what was annoying was not only its volume, but its insistence) *Dreeewww! Dreeewww! Drewww!* (the way even you are growing tired of reading it) *Dreww! Dreww!* (but it would continue until you were finally standing...) *Dreewww! Dreewwwwww!!!* (...in front of her).

Now that I am older, her voice does not call me from out of the

yard. Instead it calls me from out of sleep. I am certain I have dreamed no other voice so often as I have dreamed my mother's. It is that way in which we dream the sounds that surround us, and in this way my mother has transformed many of my dreams into nightmares. Whenever I am home my mother doesn't care if I am dreaming of the most fantastic act of acrobatic sex – her voice will still be resounding in that oneiric landscape: *DRREEEWWW! DREEEEWWWWW!* Until finally I flutter my eyes open to see her, fully dressed and standing above me, with her handbag, and seemingly oblivious to the fact that the bedside clock says it is not even six in the morning. "Come, come, come!" My mother demanded the last time I was home. "Take me to the bank now! I need to get there before the lines!"

3. The Sweet Mouth

As a child, what made me afraid of my mother's "volume" was how it attached itself quite easily to her anger. Her anger was biblical, and her arrival at home each evening would have us cowering, wondering which item was she going to find out of place this time, which dish broken, which task undone would have her bellowing our names for all and sundry to hear – this anger always out of proportion to the supposed misdemeanour she had spotted. But maybe Larkin was right: our parents always have their own issues and demons for which they should have sought therapy long ago instead of inflicting them on us. There are too many memories of my mother screaming unreasonably, and if nostalgia is the pot that will one day soften such memories, then they must stay for a while longer.

But as loud and explosive as her anger, as loud and explosive was her laughter. It is still an unapologetically humongous bark of a laugh. The ability to release it from her made you feel incredibly gifted, as if you were the most talented comedian in the world, as if the size of her laugh was the size of your joke. I work hard to make my mother laugh, but I don't think she struggles to do the same with me. I laugh at almost everything she says because – to steal an expression – my mother says the darndest things.

She has been unhappy recently with the new dog. My mother thinks that since dogs are not persons, they have no right to person-

alities. But they named the new dog Prince, and almost out of spite he has grown a somewhat haughty personality. He eats only brand-name food and is always demanding attention. My mother finally exclaimed: "Dat dog just have a bad case of tek-over!" and on the phone she refers to him only as "that damn take-over dog!"

Concerning another uncle who has begun to slip into senility (but for whom my mother thankfully has not given him the "until…" sentence), she calls me to relate the story of his decline. She tells me about his sister who went over to check on him. My mother describes the state she found him in. "My dear! Yu auntie find him…" she pauses, the significance of the vision overwhelms her "…she find him wearing two pairs of shorts. And you know that is where the sorrow start!"

In fact, I did not know this. I did not know that the wearing of two shorts was a clear signal of an impending calamity. But I laughed – because my mother often has this ability, of dressing up hard things in sweet words.

4. The Foul Mouth

When she was still living in Jamaica, my Aunt Clare declared to my mother one day, "That's it Elverine! That's it! I done going in any car with you!" Aunt Clare appreciated the rides my mother would give her from our house to Half-Way-Tree; she certainly didn't mind the lickle AC; and she was all too happy not to have to squash herself up on a Jamaican minibus. But she was a devout Christian and she worried that these earthly journeys, however convenient, might have repercussions on her spiritual journey. Sure, she would reach Half-Way-Tree in relative comfort, but would she reach Heaven on that great day? Such was the power of my mother's cursing whenever she went behind a car wheel that poor Aunt Clare thought God would spite everyone in the car, whether they had said the badwords or not. No way was she going to go to hell on account of one foul-mouthed sister.

In my childish mind it seemed to me my mother's language, when she drove, was full of apostrophes and ampersands and number signs and exclamation marks. When someone suddenly pulled out in front

of her without indicating, she would say: *What de @#!!% &#!^* and when someone slammed on their brakes suddenly, she would bellow: *But kuh pon dis @#!!% &#!^%^&# #$@*.

Now, my mother did not curse like a sailor. Such an analogy doesn't help. My mother cursed exactly like herself – like who she was – a decent, middle-class, Jamaican woman from Hope Pastures who still goes to Church every Sunday she can manage. It was those stinking bad drivers who drew out her tongue, so to speak, and the drawing out of her tongue not only surprised my aunt Clare; not only surprised the offending driver; sometimes it seemed to surprise my mother! When a driver had done something utterly reckless on the road and my mother had shouted "Yu fucking pussyhole!" she would then turn to us and quickly apologize, "Lawd mi children, don't mind, don't mind…", and then recognizing that this asshole of a driver had made her curse such crude words in front of her two good good pickney, she would be offended all over again, step on the gas, pull up beside the other car, roll down her window, push her head out and declare once more, "Yu fucking pussyhole!"

MAKING SPACE FOR GRIEF

Grief is a country we all must visit, and it helps to know
what it's like there, how others have survived
the journey, the maps they followed
— Joanne Lynn

My mother recently accompanied me on a two-week trip overseas.
I did not expect it of her. I had been invited with a few other
writers to go on the kind of tour that ought to give us pause. It
was a "disaster tour" and so certain questions peppered my mind:
Was this just another way to exploit the ailing? Would this just
be more privileged people picking their ways through the rubble
and feeling fantastically moved by the devastation and the heroism
of the poor? But these disasters weren't always recent, and so in
a way it was more a tour of history – thinking about how places
had risen and fallen. We were, too, mostly people from poor places
visiting a much more prosperous land. We were from the developing
world – Kenya, Jamaica, the Philippines, Burma, Bosnia. The country
we were visiting was America.

As for my mother coming along, it was not simply that I doubted
she would be up for the challenge – a fortnight of living on buses and
in airport lounges. There were her years of illness to be taken into
consideration, and the dialysis she had to do twice a week. But even
if she had been ready to roll up her jeans and walk through the various
landscapes touched by hurricanes or oil-spills or recessions or civil
wars, I still did not expect it of her for the simple reason that she was
dead.

I admit, however, that I may have been the one to summon her. I
did not do it on purpose and, since then, realise I have to be careful
of the first conversation I have when arriving in a new place. First
conversations have a way of framing everything else.

I had flown in to Baltimore from Glasgow and it was after

midnight when I landed. There is something about airports in the early hours that reminds me of hospitals – the large, stark whiteness of it all; the surly janitor vacuuming; the drawn faces of loved ones waiting. My old friend, Hugh Ferrer, had organized the trip and it was his face that greeted me. We got sandwiches and sat down while waiting on the car to take us through to Gettysburg. I looked at Hugh and thought, *He hasn't changed.* It hadn't been that long to be honest. He was still tall (which I guess is unchangeable) and still blond and still lanky. I knew the foot-long sandwich he had ordered would be lost without a trace in the vortex of his fast metabolism. My sandwich would become part of the five or so extra pounds I was resigned to gaining while in America. Hugh wanted to know what had been happening in the three years since we had seen each other, so I told him about the job, and about the PhD, and finally that my mother had died.

"I'm sorry," Hugh offered.

"Thanks."

I looked out the large windows of the airport into the night of Baltimore. Black porters wearing heavy windbreakers were helping passengers into taxis and shuttles. I turned back to Hugh. It had occurred to me suddenly that this was someone with whom I could risk honesty. So I told him something strange.

"I haven't cried yet. Two years, and I haven't cried. It's like I've been so busy observing myself, I feel as if nothing I do will ever be authentic – like maybe I'll just be performing grief and not really feeling it."

I told him how I had gone back to Jamaica for the funeral. A family friend had been waiting at the gate of my parents' house. His arms opened when he saw me and his face creased with pity. "My God. My God," he kept on saying.

I remember hating this family friend for his greeting, for what he expected from me – that I should become weak with grief in his arms, that I should begin sobbing onto his breast. "Yeah, it sucks," I said, and walked right by him and into the house.

I told Hugh all of this. It was the first conversation I had in America, and just like that my mother showed up, and she did on that trip what the dead do so well – she haunted it.

<div align="center">★</div>

I took photographs of rusted oil rigs and collapsed roofs and the

watermarks high up on the house walls of New Orleans – watermarks that said all too poignantly: people drowned here. I scribbled notes, little impressions, reminders of bigger stories, like the note that said simply – "Woman screaming at fallen bottle in Downtown, Baltimore."

We had just returned to Baltimore from the necropolitan landscape of Gettysburg. The downtown buildings seemed to glow white in the sun and I went out walking. After just twenty minutes I had found myself at the Old Lexington Market. Looking around, I thought: *Here is a place where I should fit in – a place far away from white America.* And maybe that is the reason I felt all the more conspicuous – because, despite my black skin and dreadlocks, I was suddenly aware of my not-baggy-enough, nor low-hanging-enough jeans; aware of my lack of "swag"; aware of my recently acquired British vocabulary – "Cheers" and "Ta" which I couldn't help but offer to people as I squeezed by them, and the unfortunate habit of using the adverb "rather" rather too often.

I walked from wooden stall to wooden stall. I tried not to stay so short a time that it would seem impolite, nor so long a time that the vendor would ask, "What you want, son?" But when I spotted a long, snaking line for crab cakes, I decided to join it. This was not because I was hungry but because someone had told me that if there was one thing I ought to eat in Baltimore it was a crab cake.

I soon noticed something peculiar about the woman standing in front of me. It was hard not to. She never moved forward unless someone else shouted at her. Even then it was usually not until the second or third shout. She was humming to herself as well, a single indecipherable note, and clutching a brown paper bag. She clutched the bag so tight that it revealed the shape of its contents – a bottle. Occasionally the paper-bag would fall from her hands, and this would surprise her. She would look to the floor and begin shouting, even wailing. In a slow and lumbering way, she would finally bend to pick up the bottle that miraculously never broke and the process would start all over.

"Grief and calamity!" a distinctly Jamaican voice whispered. It was my mother standing behind me. She said it with her lips pouted, shaking her head in the way that Caribbean women of her generation will do – a sad sort of judgement.

'What yu mean?' I asked.

She continued looking at the woman, shaking her head with a deep pity. "Grief and calamity," she said again, as she would say in New Orleans, and then in Alabama, and then again on the coastline of Louisiana.

<center>★</center>

"Disaster" is not the most euphemistic word for death but it is a euphemism all the same. All these places were somehow trying to make sense of the fact that people and things around them had either died or were dying. What seemed incredible to me was that in every place people were not only experiencing grief, but they were also making a space for it. In Gettysburg Park the historians were on the constant lookout for trees. Whenever new ones sprang up they would order it cut down. "We need to preserve the land," one of them explained to me. "We must keep it the way it was during the battle."

"Oh," I said, though it seemed strange to me – to lock a landscape forever into its mourning, even while it tried to heal itself.

The birds in New Orleans had also created grief spaces – fields of sunflowers all over the city. An old woman explained to me. "Seems the birds panicked during the hurricane and just dropped sunflower seeds everywhere."

Grief, then, had its own architecture. Or maybe it has several kinds of architecture. It occurred to me that one could either lose oneself feeling and being overwhelmed by grief, or one could get busy building a proper space for it. One could get busy thinking about the right nails, boards and roofs.

When my mother died, my neighbour in Scotland said "Oh dear!" and then as if to live up to all the stereotypes of Britishness, she asked, "Would you like a cup of tea?" But a teacup is not an appropriate space for grief. Teacups hold grief just as incompetently as they hold storms. Another kind of architecture is necessary.

<center>★</center>

After ten days I was tired. We were sitting in yet another airport lounge, six of us scattered around, stretched out on seats without obstructions between them, or on the floor. I sat watching or remembering my dead mother massage her swollen legs.

Vicente came over and sat beside me. He was from the Philippines – a quiet and reserved man. I didn't turn around to him.

"Is it your mother, again?" he asked gently.

I nodded.

"Why do you think you're seeing her?"

I shrugged at first, and then turned to him and told him what I had told Hugh. "Maybe it's that then. That I haven't cried about it yet."

Vicente's usual reserve vanished. His face contorted itself in a mask of surprise. "But how could you not cry!?" he demanded.

I turned back around and watched a small plane taxi toward its gate. The airport intercom sounded and a robotic voice announced that we should keep our belongings secure at all times. Vicente had softened by this point. "I'm sorry," he said. "And I know what you mean actually. It was almost the same with me when my grand-mother died. I didn't react at first. But… but then I had to say something at her funeral, and I guess I just broke." He smiled at this memory. "I cried. I mean, I really cried, and it was beautiful."

I swallowed something in my throat and should have told him something else – how I too came to the verge of such a moment.

At my mother's funeral I was asked to say something. I thought if there was anything I could do for her I could at least say something beautiful. But also, it had to be funny. That it is how it was with us. Any time I thought of a joke I would call my mother in Jamaica and share it, knowing that she would laugh so loudly and so scandalously that the neighbours would hear and would hardly believe that this woman in the house next door was ill and had been in bed for years.

So I read this thing at her funeral – this funny thing – and people laughed the way I wanted them to laugh. And then, near the end, my voice stumbled as if the thing I was reading was not funny at all. My voice stumbled all the way towards breaking and I had to take several breaths before I could continue. It was too late for everyone else. Everyone who had been laughing was now crying. I stood there and watched them.

Later, back at the house while the goat was being curried and the mannish water was being cooked, and while everyone was settling into their hushed little groups, I stood by a tree just watching it all.

An aunt came over to me. "It was a beautiful thing that you did today," she said, holding my hand. "You made me cry."

I smiled and hugged her. Still it seemed a strange compliment – all the more strange coming from her who had been crying from the moment she came off the plane. She was dry-eyed now. She let go of my hand but kept looking in my eyes, "It was a beautiful thing you did. An important thing."

And I wondered if this was something else about grief I was just learning – that if it is inside of us, we want someone to hold us tight and squeeze it out so that it is no longer a thing in our throats or behind our eyes or in our bellies. No. We do not want grief inside us; we would rather be inside of grief. We would rather know grief as a space that we can enter, and then leave.

<div align="center">★</div>

My fortnight in America had begun in Gettysburg – the sunlight of that first morning revealing the sprawl of the Civil War cemetery. I went jogging past the tombstones and the obelisks and the statues. I noted how perfect the grass was.

The two weeks ended beside another cemetery – the most famous in America – Arlington. I wondered about that – these graveyards like parentheses on either end of the trip.

On our penultimate day in America we had a public debriefing at the American University in Washington DC. Eduardo Halfon sat on the stage, his tonsure reflecting the big lights that were above him. Eduardo, not by virtue of age, but by virtue of a kind of nervousness that needed always to know that we were where we should be and that everyone was okay, had become the virtual father of the group. We had teased him by occasionally asking him the stupid little things that a child might. "Eduardo, can we please use the bathroom? Eduardo, can we please have a candy?" or better still, "Eduardo, are we there yet!?"

On stage, Eduardo was trying to summarise our experience from Baltimore to Alabama. He did a good job, though in the end he appeared suddenly lost as if in a trance. The refrain he kept coming back to, the question he posed that he couldn't answer himself, was "Why us? Why writers?"

Again and again he asked it. *Why us? Why writers?* Soon he was pulling us all into this trance. I began thinking it was probably more important that we couldn't yet answer this question. I began thinking about my notebook filled with notes, and my camera's memory card

filled with pictures, and all the thoughts that had been circling and circling round my head. And it suddenly seemed to me that I was being so goddamned contemplative and trying to be so goddamned smart, and not allowing myself to just be overwhelmed.

The two weeks had been that. Overwhelming. It had been an incredible and a perplexing sojourn, an uplifting and a heartbreaking journey. But in the end none of it made sense as a whole. I couldn't find a single narrative that had been running through everything – from the empty and crumbling Victorian houses of Baltimore; to the empty lots of New Orleans; to the story of the flustered birds that had dropped sunflower seeds all over the city after the hurricane; to the house that we had stood across from in Birmingham that had once belonged to Herschell Hamilton, "the bite doctor", a physician who had treated those who had been bitten by dogs during the Civil Rights demonstrations of 1963. Here at the end I was confronted with a kaleidoscope of images and realized that they didn't all go together. I thought of my small notes that were supposed to remind me of bigger stories; I thought of the hundreds of pictures I had taken; I thought about my mother, but there was no narrative – no story. There was just the overwhelm.

Months later I would still be thinking these thoughts – about grief and writers trying to make sense of it. Why us indeed? Why writers? And I think I now know.

Eduardo, if I may: I think it is because we are elegists. Which is just another way of saying we are in the business of creating spaces for grief. There are not many people who do this kind of work, who are willing to face such bleak visions and write it down, and so we must.

Eduardo, do you remember Charlie Duff, who we met in Baltimore, a silver-haired man who kept on telling us to "Look! Ask yourself, what is happening here?" Charlie Duff had trained to be a city planner but had become a developer instead, and of the most rare kind – a developer with a soul. It would probably be more accurate to say that Charlie had become a reviver. He brought dead parts of his city back into life. But even Charlie would point out streets that would never come back to life. That is what he said, and we would hear these exact words a few days later in New Orleans. An old

woman on a bus would point to abandoned hospitals and abandoned malls and abandoned neighbourhoods and she would tell us with a sad finality: *That is never coming back.*

Eduardo, I think that whenever something vanishes – a person or a place, that someone ought to create a grief space – not for what is lost, but for those of us who have the loss. Before our trip I never fully appreciated that places could die like people. I thought that if a place died that it would do so slowly, gradually. I never knew that a place could die right in front of our eyes, even as we held onto its hand, as if we were sitting by the bedside of our ailing mothers.

Eduardo, New Orleans is dead. It was washed away by an escaped lake. A new city is now growing where the old one had been, and the new city will keep the name. At least this time around, the name will be true, as John Biguenet assures us that this brand new New Orleans is not the one he grew up in.

Eduardo, the bayous are dead. Over one hundred of these magnificent swamps are buried permanently under the roads and the highways that the government thought were more important. And even if I were to take up a pickaxe right now and destroy those many miles of asphalt, the bayous and their birds and their alligators would not come back.

Eduardo, there are whole streets in Baltimore that are dead. The houses on these streets are empty and not even squatters will move in. The boards on their windows will not come down until the houses themselves fall. These streets will sink into the earth like Ancient Egypt, waiting for an archaeologist to rediscover it a thousand years from now.

Eduardo, the coast of Louisiana is dying. It is drowning every day as if it was a weary swimmer that could not manage another stroke. The landscape changes; it diminishes so quickly that cartographers cannot keep up. The lost bits of coast are never coming back. They have become a past tense.

Eduardo, my mother is dead. I imagined her on this trip, but she really wasn't. She is gone. And what can we do about any of this but write elegies? What can we do but create grief spaces, in our own small ways?

That is why us, Eduardo. That is why writers.

★

On the final day of the trip to America, before packing and going to the airport, I made sure to put the "Do not disturb" sign on the door of my hotel room. I realized that there was a grief space I had created some time ago and it was now time for me to re-enter it.

I opened my computer and searched for the thing I had written for my mother's funeral. I read it aloud, smiling, and then chuckling. And at the point when my voice broke, as it did two years before, I did not stop it from breaking. I allowed it to tumble all the way down. I allowed myself into a grief space.

As I sobbed into the carpet, my mother patted my back. "Grief and calamity," she whispered with something that sounded like pride. "Grief and calamity."

<div align="center">★</div>

REMEMBRANCE FOR A LION-HEARTED WOMAN
Vivette Elverine Miller (1947 – 2009)

When the phone rang at five in the morning, I wondered who it was. And then I wondered if it was my sister, and then I wondered if my mother had died. There was no real reason to think this. The dogs upstairs were not howling. My mother had not just visited me in a dream, nor had I been dreaming of a wedding. But just ten days before, I stood by her bed and watched her sleeping. I waited to be sure her chest was still filling itself. And right there, I said a prayer for her. And if this phone call meant what I had begun to think it might mean, this phone that had always fit so easily in my hands, seemed heavy – the heaviest thing I would ever lift.

And as I walked to the phone thinking about her – my mother who has fought so hard to stay alive, but has spent the greater part of these last five years in bed, flicking through channels, watching *The Price is Right* – I think maybe it is time to fit the words of Jesus into my mouth and tell her, and insist, *Rise, woman, rise. Get up and walk.* And so I hope it is her on the other end of the line, and realize suddenly, it may well be, because she has done this before, woken me up at five in the

morning, fully dressed, saying *Come, come, come, I need to go to the bank before the lines get too bad!*

Wherever you were, at whatever time of day you got that awful call, I suspect you did exactly what I did. We all did it instinctively, because we do not know how to perform bigger miracles. Our magic is rudimentary, so we simply remembered her. We raised her up in our memories because this is the only way we know to bring people back. At first, it wasn't anything magnificent that we remembered. Just the small things – the last time we spoke, the sound of her voice; the last time we saw her, the sound of her voice; the way she fought, but always the sound of her voice; the roar of her laughter, this lion that was inside her.

There are parts we will not want to remember. The last years were hard, the last weeks especially. When she thought no one was nearby, she would cry. She would rock herself and repeat over and over, *Please Jesus, Please Jesus.* I think she wanted answers. She did not want to be sick; she did not want to die; she did not think it fair. The lion inside kept baring its teeth, growling at death to stay back.

Other memories are easier. The way for instance she was surprisingly generous at times – the kind of woman to put money into an envelope, and quietly press that envelope into the hands of someone she decided needed it.

Or the way she would come alive when reading a Miss Lou poem, the way she could step completely into the skin of a street peddler or "dat old gal Liza" or Nephew Sue. My mother despaired at times of her middle-class children (in particular her daughter) who, despite coaching, could never get de sounds exactly right. This was one of the few things she accepted blame for – *We send de child to Canada when she was young, and she come back in body but de accent still someplace else.*

She was less magnanimous regarding almost everything else. My mother was that strange combination of an organized woman who lost things, and when she lost things she could not accept that it was her own self who had misplaced it. She would call one of us, hell and heaven in her voice, demanding who had moved the remote, or her scrabble set,

or whatever it was, because *Dese tings can't just get up demself and walk!* And if, duly irritated, we set out to prove our innocence by searching for the item, finding it, and putting it back into her hands, her ungracious thanks was either a begrudging "Hm!" or a particularly cutting, "Is you did put it dere."

She liked colours and fabric and clothes. It was a rare occasion when she let more than twenty-four hours pass before wearing an outfit she had just bought. She prided herself on the ability to put herself together well, and appropriately.

Like every couple, there were ways in which my parents were quite opposites, but most profoundly they were opposites when it came to the matter of time. Mom always wanted to be early, Dad was always late. The later Dad was the more Mom's anger would grow, the lion inside her stretching its paws. But there was one occasion on which Dad managed to completely, even if unwittingly, defuse this anger and tame the lion. Mom had been ready and waiting and waiting to go out to some event. It may have been a cricket match. It couldn't have been something very formal because she had decided on an elegantly casual ensemble. Dad finally arrived and before his wife could start shouting, he looked on her, confused, and said, "Vivette, you not going to get ready," to which my mother's suddenly quiet, if not slightly stunned response was, "Yes, dear, I was just about to."

I put these memories together, her love of colour and clothes, the sound of her voice – how loud it was; and I realize one of her faults (yes, she had a couple) may have been her love of attention. She liked people doting on her. This is why I know she does not approve of Michael Jackson dying just three days after she did. She does not like this division of grief. She does not like that the newspapers are talking about his golden coffin, and the elephants that will bear him up. She wonders why, just for this one moment, the world might not celebrate her?

So we must tell her: Mom, we do. We have come from Spanish Town, and St. Ann and St. Mary and Uptown and Downtown to be with you. We have travelled on planes to be

here. We have come from New York and Delaware and Florida, and we have come from Bahamas and Canada and Scotland. Right here, right now, you are the centre of the world's attention. Because, in the only way we know how to do such things, we perform a miracle. We call you forth like Lazarus. We remember you. And forgive us if we do it too late, but right now, in our memories, we command you, at last, to rise.

WHAT NAMES RECALL
(2010)

I'm driving from the city of Glasgow into the Scottish Highlands.
I am passing the names of towns and villages – Braehead, Inverness,
Glencoe – and thinking about how these names remember the
landscape and how sometimes they recall the past back into the
present. Names often do this kind of thing.

I am thinking of a place in Jamaica called Swamp. Developers
began to build houses there in 2003 but after everything that hap-
pened had happened, some turned around and said: *Well, how
ridiculous was that, to build houses in a place called Swamp.* The
developers were defensive. *How were we to know? The place hadn't
been a swamp for 70 years!* And I think – maybe that was it – that the
place and its name had been forgotten, but now everyone had begun
to recall it, had begun saying, *I am building a house in Swamp*; or, *I am
living in Swamp*; or, *have you seen the lovely, large houses in Swamp?*
Over and over. Swamp, swamp, swamp. So the place finally remem-
bered its past, remembered its swampish landscape, and before you
could say "hurricane season" or "tropical weather conditions" or
"flash flood warnings", those large, lovely houses ended up at the
bottom of a swamp. The developers, trying to recoup some of their
money, put up a Ferris wheel on the bank of the waters and offered
boat rides to tourists who came – pouring in, as it were. The tour
guides on the boats would say: *Welcome to Moneague. Welcome to
Swamp. We are now sailing over an avenue, and now we are sailing across
a boulevard; yes, my dears, underneath us is a line of twelve two-storey
houses, twelve back gardens, and many many yards of soaked carpet.* The
tourists in turn would look vainly into the murk underneath the
glass-bottomed boat, and say *Ooooh!* imagining the community
below like a little Atlantis.

I grew up in a community called Hope Pastures and I think now,
maybe it was the name that recalled the cows each morning. We

accept as natural the things that we grow up seeing, so I never thought it odd to a live in a place that said it was suburban, but where cows would trot up and down the road as they pleased. They trampled our fences, came into our yards and ate the grass. And who could blame them? This was supposed to be pasture land after all. We were never surprised to be greeted each morning by steaming cow pats in our driveways.

I grew up, more specifically, on a street called Forsythe Drive and this recalls a man by the name of Reverend Forsythe, which in turn recalls a wonderful story about mangoes. Reverend Forsythe, it is said, once ate three entire carts of mangoes just to prepare himself for an eating competition later that day. When Banging John, his competition, saw these donkey carts full of mango seeds and heard that this was just preparation, and knew that his own belly, massive as it was, was nowhere as big as three carts, he ran away. Hope Pastures used to be a mango walk, and I imagine that this Reverend Forsythe ate his mangoes somewhere on what is now Forsythe Drive. I imagine this because there are many mango trees in the back of my parents' house and some of them are so sweet you feel as if you could eat entire cartloads of them.

I live now in a place called Whiteinch. The "inch" here is not a measurement but an old Scots word for Island. The name Whiteinch recalls a time when this bit of land was not on the bank of the River Clyde but in the middle of it. That I have bought a piece of a Presbyterian Church in a place called Whiteinch recalls my deep attraction to islands and to God. One day I fully expect to wake up surrounded by a mighty river.

The name I have used for the past ten years is Kei. This recalls my father. It is the name he was called at UWI in the days when he was active in the guild and the occupying students locked themselves for months in the Creative Arts Centre. The name Kei recalls Walter Rodney and a time of protest. It recalls its own missing letters, the "T" and the "H'" that have run away from its end. So Kei recalls a time when it did not rhyme with "sky", but with "sea". My first name however is Andrew which recalls my sister who at the age of four was given the solemn duty of choosing a name for her brother. My name, Andrew, recalls Vaz Preparatory School; it recalls two boys that my sister liked – Richard and Andrew. It recalls important decisions that

occasionally have to be made by children; it recalls the unworthiness of Richard; it recalls the faith of parents; it recalls the fact that a four-year old girl's affection is ever-shifting.

The name Kei recalls ink and paper and the hard decision to be a writer at a time when other friends were deciding to be lawyers and doctors – things that would put food on the table. I do not mind being called Andrew. Most people who love me and who have known me from the days long before still call me Andrew. I am annoyed however (thought I try not to show it) when people refer to me as Andrew Miller – the writer. This isn't a rejection of my name, it's just that I think it isn't Andrew who is the writer. This isn't the name on any of my books. I also think that Kei is in fact a very different person from Andrew, and the strength of this belief makes me wonder if all writers really are a little schizophrenic.

The name that my friends call me is Dready which recalls my youth. It recalls a time when my hair touched the blades of my shoulders. When I cut my hair off at the age of thirty, because I had said to myself – well that's it, my youth is officially over, my friends did not stop calling me Dready. I think it is the fact that they did not stop calling me this that called me back from baldness. It brought my hair back into being.

And sometimes in Jamaica I will be walking in the plazas and someone will call out, "Rice!" I always turn around and smile. "How have you been since Moorlands?" I say. The person will exclaim, "Wow! I can't believe you remember." In truth, I usually do not remember, but this is just what the name Rice recalls. It recalls Mandeville and Moorlands Camp. It recalls Top House and Sundays where I used to cry and was broken; it recalls prophecy; it recalls a time when I believed in things I wish, every day, I still believed in.

My best friend is called Smiley, and there are days when I am jealous of this. I wonder if he is always called back to happiness even in days that are relentlessly dark.

I am driving from the city of Glasgow into the Scottish Highlands. I am passing all these wonderful names of towns, names that recall the mouths of rivers and waterfalls and languages hardly spoken again and the seasonal passage of animals. I'm thinking of my own name, Miller, and how it has recalled me to this new country in which I now live.

A SMALLER SOUND, A LESSER FURY – A EULOGY FOR DUB POETRY

In characteristic Mervyn Morris style, the distinguished professor sets out a definition for dub poetry that is as careful as it is (by virtue of its many allowances) incontestable. He says:

> "Dub poetry", which is written to be performed, incorporates a music beat, often a reggae beat. Often, but not always, the performance is done to the accompaniment of music, recorded or live. Dub poetry is usually, but not always, written in Jamaican language; in Jamaican Creole (dialect, vernacular, nation language). By extension, it may be written in the informal language of people from anywhere. Most often it is politically focused, attacking oppression and injustice. Though the ideal context for dub poetry is the live performance, it also makes itself available in various other ways: on radio, on television, in audio recordings, video recordings and on film. Many dub poets also publish books.[1]

My own thoughts which follow are not so carefully laid out. They might even seem to beg for contestation. This is not an attempt to stir things up gratuitously; if I paint with large and sometimes abstract strokes, I still hope that the final image on the canvas will depict a general truth.

At the heart of this essay is a hypothesis about diasporas and how they work – about how things which die a certain kind of death within the "home" society are sometimes preserved in the diaspora. I have thought for a while that a more creative anthropologist, curious about the things which a certain culture might lose naturally over a few generations, would be able to find those things largely intact within the diaspora. I've walked through Brixton, and in certain parts of Birmingham, and in Manchester, and have heard snippets of speech from West Indian immigrants, and often times it employs a lexicon that is very much from the Caribbean but which is no longer

heard there. And also, in observing the fashion on display, sometimes you are able to tell when it was that a person might have left – because their clothes are still preserving that time, like mementos of their leaving. Consider, for instance, that most outstanding of dub poets, Linton Kwesi Johnson, and what has become his signature look – the felt hat, the sharp tweed suit – all of which announce a West Indian of a particular era. In the diaspora there seems a natural unwillingness to let go of things which are seen as synonymous with home. So although these things might slip away or even die in their original contexts, in the diaspora they are preserved. If you are flabbergasted that I should sing the death of something that is still practised in certain quarters – can still be heard on certain stages – that brand of performance poetry that came out of Jamaica – you might consider this central hypothesis – that the life that some things lead within diasporas is a kind of mummified life.

A Mytho-poetic Account of the Birth of Dub Poetry

Oku Onuora, whose original name was Orlando Wong, is often given the progenitive title, "father of dub poetry". The title is also sometimes passed on to Bongo Jerry, to Mutabaruka and also to Linton Kwesi Johnson. Genres and forms, of course, do not start in isolation and are never usually the product of any one individual, but as this is a mytho-poetic account, Orlando Wong is as good a place to start as any.

He was imprisoned between 1970 and 1977 for armed robbery. Importantly, this indiscretion has been recast in popular narrative as a Robin Hood kind of a crime; he stole from the rich to give to the poor. Wong allegedly had held up a post office in order to fund a community project. I do not mean to suggest that an altruistic motive really wasn't behind Wong's crime, but of course the narrative of an event is sometimes more important than the event itself, and how we imagine facts is sometimes more powerful than the facts themselves. Already, Wong was being reformed into a hero – a champion of the poor.

They say it was in prison that Wong began writing what would become known as dub poetry and started becoming popular for it.

Through the intervention of one Leonie Forbes he had even established contact with Mervyn Morris, who became something of a regular visitor. They say, however, that things almost ended as soon as they had begun. After an early performance of Wong's poetry it was found to be so subversive, and had such a rallying effect, that his writing book was confiscated and he was forbidden to write anymore.

But in Jamaica things are neither kept in or out of prison (not even prisoners) and there is a regular trafficking of items – cigarettes, guns, women – between outside and inside. Orlando Wong not only continued writing, but his poems (and indeed his very self) were trafficked out into a society then caught up in the heady excitement of Black Power. The timing was perfect. People found in Wong's poems a poetry that was railing against oppression, railing against social injustice, and that had the credibility of being composed inside and coming directly out of a Jamaican prison. This was the voice of the black underclass. And if there was any concern at his Chinese surname (I do not know that there was) he would soon go to deed-poll and change it to something suitably Afro-centric.

Support built for Wong's release from prison and at last the government led by Michael Manley offered him a full pardon. And because we can do no worse, and because we can hardly be more specific in such matters, let us call this the moment when conception officially happened, when Jamaica and the spirit of revolution and the rhythms of reggae and the cries against injustice and the realities of prison all fertilized each other. Imagine then the labour as the day when the prison gates opened on 1st September 1977, the day when dub poetry was officially born into the world. Orlando Wong named himself Oku Onuora, and he named this thing that he was writing dub poetry.

In narrating its birth, however, I may have already begun to hint at some of the reasons dub poetry would eventually die – or if not "die" completely, at least it would "die down". Dub poetry was the voice of a revolution and revolutions do not last forever. There are, for this reason, revolutionaries who have found themselves out of work, fighters desperately looking for a war to fight. The Jamaican dub poet Klyde Broox has already written to me – all sound and fury, as it were – upset at my suggestion that dub poetry is not as alive today as it was in the '70s or the '80s. Some concession must be made here

– for Broox is writing out of Canada, a space and a scene which he knows much more intimately than I do. And yet, Broox seems not to fully understand my argument, for if my point was simply that dub poetry has seen a natural falling off over the years, I would be fighting a straw man. The case is almost incontestable, the dubious exception of Canada notwithstanding. Or maybe the concept of "death" is too stark and final to describe what is more accurately a "dying down" or a "dying away". But you might allow me some poetic licence here. And my point is not so much to pronounce the death (or the dying down) of the form, but to perform a sort of autopsy and figure out why and when its life began to ebb, and also why it is that some of us insist on propping up the corpse. Broox, by all accounts, and indeed from my own experience, is a generous spirit and the most conscientious of activists. Broox probably feels himself attacked, or else called on to defend the movement he has committed his life to. He probably thinks that to sound the death knell of a movement is the same as diminishing the importance of that movement. After all, revolutionary fighters do not want to find that they are out of work because the revolutions they championed have ended; nor do they wish to discover that a whole new nuclear war has begun while they have been continuing the fight uselessly with outdated muskets. And this may be part of the problem – that poets such as Broox, and others who earnestly and uncritically wave the flag of dub poetry today, don't seem to have the poetic arsenal to insist on the thriving power of the art form in which they work.

If I were to write a dub poem

Back in Jamaica, I am watching a newscast and see probably the most traumatic thing I have ever seen on television. Viewer discretion is advised but this hardly prepares me. The news footage is of a very thin man wearing only a small pair of shorts. His black skin has become white with dust as if he has lived for months under a chalkboard; he is in fact rolling about on the marl ground, shivering. Three police officers look on and they have their batons raised and use these to occasionally beat the man.

The man is not of sound mind. Apparently, he has not long ago

stabbed his wife to death. In this moment of footage, however, he is no longer the aggressor. He is at the mercy of the three officers who have taken it as their duty to punish him. The community – his neighbours – who are looking on and angry at what his psychotic meltdown has caused – are cheering on the officers.

And then it happens: one police officer begins to threaten the man. You cannot hear what he is saying from the footage (all of this is being recorded on a camera phone), but you notice how the sergeant cocks his head upward and begins to mouth what seem to be slow and dangerous words. The crowd cheers even louder, and this you can hear. The police officer, as if energized by the crowd, now reaches into his belt and raises his gun instead of his baton. He walks a full circle around the man, like something out of a mafia film, then points his gun directly at the man's head and pulls the trigger.

Sometimes the human body does strange things when it knows it is about to die. This was not the kind of gunshot death I had ever seen in movies. The man's body lurches violently and desperately underneath a car as if it would be safe there. And then the footage ends.

Maybe that is a strange thing to put into the middle of this essay, but an obvious thing occurred to me as I watched that news footage – the kind of thing that should occur to most of us many times a week: that there will always be things in this world that we should be shouting about; that there will always be injustices both in the wide world, and in our particular worlds; that there will always be placards that need writing; and that although revolutions end, new ones ought to spring up every morning; that though dub poetry today makes such a faint sound, the need for a poetry with the same kind of conscience has never diminished.

We need voices of protest in Jamaica, and in Brixton, and in Toronto. It is just that dub poetry too often seems to shape today's hurt and pain into yesterday's voice and image – the shape of the '70s. The oppressor, however, is no longer that easy category of the "white man". Too often I have been to readings and heard my generation – we who are the children of the rebels of the '70s, with our posh education, with our dreadlocks that have never had us thrown out of the house – chanting down Babylon with a blissful unawareness that we have in fact become Babylon, that we have become implicated in this system of oppression, and that our dark skins do not make us

innocent of anything. And while I do not want to glorify the kind of
art that is borne out of hardships, there is something about Oku
Onuora's poetry, coming out of prison, and something about Linton
Kwesi Johnson's poems, narrated as they were on the edge of the riots
in Brixton – there is something that they can affect that my own
generation often don't get right. There is something lost in volume
and potency when we try to mimic a sound rather than create our
own, fashioned out of our own introspection and pain; when my
generation attempts dub poetry it seems to always come out as a
smaller sound, and a lesser fury.

When Dub Poetry Made A Greater Sound

Let us consider two dub poems.
 Mikey Smith's "Me Cyaan Believe It" takes us on a tour around
Jamaica in the 1970s and gives us a catalogue of injustices, inequalities
and hardships. All of them are commented on with the remark – Me
Cyaan Believe It.

> Me seh me cyaan believe it
> me seh me cyaan believe it
>
> room dem a rent
> me apply widin
> but as me go een
> cockroach rat an scorpion
> also come een
>
> Waan good
> nose haffi run
> but mi naw go siddun pon high wall
> like Humpty Dumpty
> me a face me reality[2]

The lament "Me cyaan believe it" is of course rhetorical. The
persona isn't turning his eyes away from these things. In the words
of the poem he is facing his reality and asking us to face it too.
The poem asks us to lose our innocence in the same way that it
incorporates so many nursery rhymes: "Humpty Dumpty",
"Bapsikaisico pinda shell", "the little boy who blew his horn",

"the blackbirds baked in a pie" and forces them to also lose their
innocence. Even the nursery rhymes are called in to bear witness
to the things which can hardly be believed. One of my favourite
moments in the poem is the interaction between the "bwoy" and
his employer.

> De odder day
> me a pass one yard pon de hill
>
> When me teck a stock me hear
> 'Hey, bwoy!'
> 'Yes, mam?'
> 'Hey, bwoy!'
> 'Yes, mam!'
> 'Yuh clean up de dog shit?'
> 'Yes, mam.'
> An me cyaan believe it[3]

Even on page we can "hear" interesting nuances in this exchange
of voices; the punctuation helps us. At the employer's first cry
of "Hey, bwoy!" He answers with a question mark. "Yes, mam?"
It seems to suggest a kind of meekness or submissiveness. But
this response isn't alert enough for the employer's liking. She
cries again, "Hey, bwoy!" And he responds now with appropriate
military attention: "Yes, mam!" Exclamation mark. Then the
humiliating question, "Yu clean up de dog shit?" The vibrancy
of his answers now drops sharply. Downgraded from the bright
exclamation mark before, we now just get a fullstop. "Yes, mam."
The denigration signalled here is not simply that the "bwoy" has
been given the menial duty of cleaning up the dogshit, but that
more than likely this isn't a "boy" at all. The Jamaican poet, Lorna
Goodison, once asked when would it be that the yard bwoy (which
is how Jamaican middle-class employers often refer to the fully
grown man employed to tend their grounds) would finally graduate
to the man that he actually is? When does the yard bwoy become
at last the yard man, and from then become the man-a-yard?

The end of Mikey Smith's poem prophetically documents a kind
of psychic fragmentation, gesturing perhaps to his own demise. The
absurd begins to happen – the persona travels from Kingston to
Jamaica; he tries to subtract twelve from a dozen and then sees his

mother in heaven. We get the plaintive cry, "Madhouse, Madhouse"
– a dreadful pronouncement over the city of Kingston every bit as
damning as Derek Walcott's "Hell is a city, much like Port of Spain".[4]
The poem finally turns to its reader and accuses us of not believing
these atrocities too – not in the rhetorical sense that the poem uses the
phrase "me cyaan believe it", but in the actual sense that maybe we
live such comfortable lives, so far away from these other existences,
that we do not need to believe or engage with matters of social
injustice and inequality.

> Yuh believe it?
> How yuh fi believe it
> when yuh laugh
> an yuh blind yuh eye to it?
>
> But me know yuh believe it
> Lawwwwwwd
> me know yuh believe it[5]

That cry lawwwwwwwwwwd was one of Mikey Smith's signature
sounds, that distended groan from the belly, a guttural and elemental
cry for all that is rotten in the state of Kingston. In Mikey Smith's
poetry was a mighty sound and a great fury.

If Smith took us on a tour of Jamaica, in "Inglan is a bitch" Linton
takes us on a tour of London. We see it through the eyes of an
immigrant barely making a living in the city. The poem is not
autobiographical. Johnson is speaking for a larger human condition.
The persona is imagined literally inside the belly of the beast –
working on the underground. But despite the circularity of his work,
this immigrant still does not know his way "around" London.

> w'en mi jus' come to Landan toun
> mi use to work pan di andahgroun
> but workin pan di andahgroun
> y'u don't get fi know your way aroun'
>
> Inglan is a bitch
> dere's no escapin' it
> Inglan is a bitch
> dere's no running whey fram it[6]

Throughout the poem the refrain changes slightly in each of its

seven invocations. It graduates from a passive acceptance, to a more active engagement, and finally to a prompt towards revolution. First we get "Inglan is a bitch, there's no running whey fram it" which seems a statement of passivity and acceptance of what England will throw at the subject. Then we get "Inlan is a bitch, noh badda try hide from it", more passivity, then "Inglan is a bitch fi true, a noh lie mi a tell, a true", which is a shift in tone. The voice of insistence is creeping in. The next refrain change is decidedly empowered – "Inglan is a bitch, you haffi know how fi survive in it", and then "Inglan is a bitch, you betta face up to it". So when we come again now to "Inglan is a bitch, there's no running whey fram it", this is not the passive acceptance of its first invocation. This is a readying for revolution. The final shift in the refrain is indeed the challenging, "Inglan is a bitch, a whey we a go do bout it?"

What happened to Dub Poetry? Death

If you hear LKJ read his poetry, particularly his dub poetry (for I am careful not to suggest that all of LKJ's poems are dub poems) you will hear an incredibly distinguished performance: one that usually refuses applause during its length; one that is never histrionic; one that is forceful, but subdued. You will also get a lesson in history. LKJ usually creates a kind of pedagogical space. He is careful to locate his poetry in a particular time and place, understanding perhaps that a newer generation growing up in contemporary and proudly multicultural British cities might not immediately understand that their freedoms were birthed out of the strain and strife that his own generation faced in a less healthy, more segregated, more racist Britain – one that demanded a poetics of sound and fury.

LKJ often divides his dub poems into three decades. He will say – these are from the '70s, these are from the '80s, these are from the '90s. It is impossible not to note that we never get dub poetry of the new millennium, as if even the poet laureate of the movement locates the genre in a time that has past – as if even he is aware of the genre's death.

I suspect – though I have never asked him – that LKJ would not

necessarily mourn dub poetry's death. If, as I have just suggested, he has become the virtual "poet laureate" of the movement, it is not a position he has always occupied willingly or happily. He has described his own "attempts to distance [him]self from the term."[7] It seems to me that Linton has often expressed weariness with the category and also with its reception. While a revolution was being announced from the podium of dub, it was too often met with an applause too loud for introspection. Black, West Indian protest poets, with all their sound and fury, were slowly being accepted as lively entertainment for a Saturday night. The genre was being fetishized and commodified by the broader culture it was trying to critique. What irony, that the very attempt to protest capitalism was being put onto the production line.

Poets such as Johnson and Jean Binta Breeze and even Benjamin Zephaniah with all his "pure greeting-card doggerel"[8] as Carolyn Cooper rightly puts it, expressed the desire to write other things and in other forms. All three have since ventured into other writing projects – essays, adult and children's novels, poetry which cannot be classified as dub. In their own ways they have broken free from a genre that could have stifled their talents by demanding they continue the same minstrel show night after night.

Another thing that might well have contributed to the death of dub poetry was dancehall and the emergence of artists such as Beenie Man, Bounty Killer, Shabba Ranks, Vybz Kartel, Mavado – names which themselves will quickly date the present essay. Over the years, songs from these artistes have become the new music of youth and rebellion and protest. While the music of the likes of Taurus Riley, Jah Cure and Gyptian makes it too much to say that reggae has died, even in its most contemporary form it lacks what we might call the "dub" or "roots" feel of the '70s. Without a proper musical source then, with its fountain of youth dried up, it is little wonder that dub poetry makes a lesser sound today than it once did.

When Mikey Smith died in 1983, stoned to death when he disturbed a political meeting in Stony Hill, Jamaica, Kamau Brathwaite, a poet receptive to the influence of dub poetics on his craft, wrote the elegiac poem "Stone: for Mikey Smith". It is a stunning and heart-breaking work – a eulogy for one of the most talented dub poets there ever was, but perhaps in its own way a eulogy for dub poetry itself. It

at once captures Mikey's voice, the sound and the fury of it, that distended elemental groan, Lawwwwwwwwwwwwwd. It documents the madness that was happening to him and laments all the poems that were not chanted, all the dub that was bleeding out of this young man, and maybe out of the entire world. The poem raises one final, angry, awful, plaintive, beautiful sound, protesting a death it could not stop from happening.

> When the stone fall that morning out of the johncrow sky
> i could not hold it brack or black it back or block it off or limp
> away or roll it from me into memory or light or rock it steady into
> night...[9]

Dub poetry will continue to live a sort of life in the diaspora, because there will always be nostalgic consumers who want to purchase the product. It will also continue to live a sort of life in Jamaica, trotted out every August for Independence Day or any other cultural celebration, where it will share a stage with Dinki Mini and Kumina and other forms we find it so hard to say goodbye to, but which also require their own eulogies. I do not think I can do an eulogy as eloquent as Brathwaite's, but here is my own small attempt:

> It was born on September 1, 1977. It walked on streets that others were afraid to walk on. It spoke on behalf of the poor and the forgotten. It made the kind of sound that is more than a sound – it is an action. It acted on things that needed to be acted upon. It went around the city of Jericho; it shouted, and walls came down – in Kingston, and in Brixton, and in Bristol. It taught us that there are times to be angry, indeed to be furious, and that fury can be composed into a thing of eloquence. It is probably not the voice of today, but it is a voice that our own should willingly resonate with. Indeed should more poetic voices today carry in them the echoes of dub, it would be a very good thing. Rest in peace, dub poetry. Walk good, and mek good duppy follow you.

End Notes

1. Mervyn Morris, "Dub Poetry?" in *Is English We Speaking and other essays* (Kingston: Ian Randle Publishers, 1999) p. 36.
2 Michael Smith, "Me Cyaan Believe It", *It A Come* (London: Race Today Publications, 1986), p. 13.
3. "Me Cyaan Believe It", p. 14.
4. Derek Walcott, "The Spoiler's Return", *The Fortunate Traveller* (New York: Farrar, Straus and Giroux, 1981), p. 57.
5. "Me Cyaan Believe It", p. 15.
6. "Inglan Is a Bitch", *Inglan Is A Bitch* (London: Race Today Publications, 1980); quotation from Tings an Times: Selected Poems (Newcastle: Bloodaxe Books, 1991), pp. 13-14.
7. Linton Kwesi Johnson, "Remembering Michael Smith" in *Caribbean Culture: Soundings on Kamau Brathwaite*. Ed Annie Paul (Kingston: UWI Press, 2007) p. 155.
8. *Noises in the Blood: Orality, Gender and the Vulgar* (Duke University Press, 1986), p. 72.
9. "Stone: for Mikey Smith", *Jah Music* (Mona: Savacou Cooperative, 1986), p. 26.

AN OCCASIONALLY DANGEROUS THING CALLED "NUANCE"
(2012)

That "America is the home of freedom"; or that Jamaica is "the most homophobic country in the world"; or that "black people are the sons and daughters of kings and queens"; or that "white people are generally racist": these are the kinds of statements to which most sensible people will roll their eyes. The problem of course is nuance – or rather the lack of it – the refusal to acknowledge complexity. Almost nothing sounds so reasonable, so fair-minded, so uncontestable, as this demand (often by the academic) for nuance. I demand it from my students all the time. In the marked-up essays that I hand back to them, the word screams from the margin, and each time with more exclamation marks behind so that by the end I am a virtual hysteric: NUANCE!!!!!!!!

But nuance can become a dangerous thing. Sometimes nuance ought to be avoided.

In a class at Glasgow, I teach Chinua Achebe's collection of essays, *Hopes and Impediments*. It is a class of postgraduate students; they are generally bright, and generally white. Sometimes this situation worries me – teaching a book by a black writer who at times accuses a white audience. I fear that the "author versus reader" dynamic will mutate into a "teacher versus class" dynamic. I fear that the class might see me as complicit with the politics of the writer (in the case of Achebe's essays, I was), and so I fear that honesty will be compromised – that the class might feel less than free to share their misgivings, and that I might feel less than free to share my misgivings over their misgivings.

When it comes to it, things are of course more nuanced than that. The class does not operate as a whole. They are divided, some more

sympathetic to Achebe's positions than others. (It is, however, generally true that the North Americans in the class are less sympathetic than the British students – make of that what you will.)

Those who were not convinced by Achebe's rants against a racist world accused him of lacking nuance. They said that he used too many generalizations and that though he did occasionally acknowledge that not all white people were like this or like that, it was still not enough – he ought to have expanded on these points.

But to invent a slightly ridiculous scenario: if a black man was to walk into a room where (let's just say) ten white people are sitting, and one was to rise from her seat and scream the word "NIGGER!" at the black man, it would seem to me a curious, even a ridiculous response if any one demanded that he acknowledge that 90% of the room did not rise from their seats and call him "nigger", that the offence came from only a 10% minority. How could the man's total and profound experience be divided by such statistics? It would be using them to try to nuance away the horribleness and the stark specificity of what happened.

In class, I veer away from Achebe's text and tell them about some of my own experiences – experiences which I am sure will not be theirs. I tell them just how much I hate having to ask for directions in the city centre of Glasgow. I have done it a few times and no matter how well-dressed I am, the response I get usually makes me feel humiliated. At best, I get a wide-eyed nervousness, the person looking up and down the road for an escape, though at least this quietness allows me the space to ask my unthreatening question for directions and then they usually relax. At other times, however, I'm not allowed the space to speak. "I'm sorry, I just don't have time for this! I'm rushing!" and then they walk away – slowly, shaking their heads. Or an even worse response: "I don't have any money! Sorry!"

But I rarely tell such stories because when I do I have to become a contortionist of sorts – I have to twist the narrative in so many ways to acknowledge that yes, yes, yes – I know not everyone is like this, and yes, yes, yes, I know *you* would never do this yourself, and yes yes yes I know it is only a minority of very stupid people. After a time, all the effort is not about relating my experience, but about trying to spare my mostly white audience from feeling accused. So I save myself the effort, and spare them the accusation, but it is sad that

people cannot speak about their experiences honestly because the audience might be too defensive to listen. It seems that the immigrant's vision of the world is a decidedly difficult one to speak or to write down.

Yet in locating myself in all of this, I know I hold dual or even multiple citizenship. I belong both to a traditionally oppressed race, and to a privileged class. It is hard to think of my life as it has been these last few years – teaching at an ancient university, travelling quite a bit – and not think about the responsibility of my "privilege". I'd like to believe I understand something of both worlds, and here is a truth I now believe: that whenever we belong to a privileged class or race or group of any kind, whenever such a group is accused of their oppressive behaviours, then they/we begin to demand "nuance" or the avoidance of "easy generalizations". We believe that this demand is fair-minded, academic, and rigorous. But it often isn't. It is often an emotional demand. In such moments we are not seeking nuance at all; rather, we are seeking absolution, forgiveness, a way out, a clause that states that *we* do not to belong to the category of wicked people being accused.

And I get it. When you hear again and again the same old accusations, you grow weary of them. You begin to roll your eyes and demand – for godsake! – tell a different story. You begin to ask for nuance. But the thing is, depending on how great the oppression is, should we really give or receive the relief of nuance? When nuance becomes a way of sweeping emotional and physical bruises, maimings, unnecessary hostilities, beatings, tortures, suicides, murders, burnt houses, forced exiles, and the whole lot of it, all under the carpet – when nuance is co-opted into the systematic denial of wrongs – then we really ought to say to "nuance": thanks, but no thanks.

Get-out clauses are not helpful when they allow us to not face ourselves – when we begin to believe that if we are not the man beating the woman, or if we are not the white person shouting nigger at the black man, or if we are not part of the mob beating those two gay men, then we are somehow innocent and that there is nothing in our behaviour or our beliefs that both contribute to, fortify or even just permit this wider system of oppression.

A year or so ago on an online forum, a Ms Manley, who I've never

met but who in every regard seems to be quite a sensible person, still managed to make an astoundingly stupid point. She suggested that if gay men in Jamaica were *really* being viciously beaten, then obviously all of them would have died by now. In her curious logic, oppression and annihilation are the same things. If you had not been annihilated then you obviously hadn't been seriously oppressed.

The lessons that women, black people, Jewish people (amongst so many other categories of oppressed people) have taught us through-out history somehow missed Ms Manley – the simple truth that oppression very often leads to creative acts of subterfuge, to marronage, to various strategies of masking and passing, and to the most amazing narratives of survival. Under the weight of oppression many people have been broken, but many others have survived. Survival in no way excuses or negates the fact of oppression. As we say in Jamaica, "What don't kill yu, mek yu stronger", but that is no reason to glory in or to excuse the things that tried to kill us. Because of historic oppressions we have inherited all manner of beautiful things – recipes, rituals, songs, dances, art, language – but none of this excuses the original oppression.

Now Ms Manley was understandably annoyed by the picture the international media have been painting of Jamaica's homophobia. The Ms Manleys of Jamaica have begun to roll their eyes in weariness and to demand nuance/complexity/another kind of story for godsake! Some people have pointed to the phenomenon of Shebada (Keith Ramsay) in Jamaican theatre, or to the obvious queer aesthetic in the supposedly hyper-masculine world of Jamaican dancehall. But all of this is to be expected! Whatever is oppressed, whatever is submerged, will find ways to bubble up and over. If you have eyes intelligent enough to see it, you will see it. What you must not do, however, the mistake you must not make, is to say that because of this bubbling over, things are not so bad after all, or that the oppression isn't as much as people make it out to be. What we must not do with "nuance" (if we are responsible people) is to let it turn the dial down on our response to things and issues that need us to make as loud a sound as possible.

Not long ago in Jamaica two boys from UTECH were set upon by a crowd of tertiary level students who had decided to teach them a

lesson in "morality". One boy managed to escape; the other ran to the security guards for protection. Unfortunately the security guards decided not to protect this boy but to teach him the same violent lesson in morality that the crowd outside were intent on.

Now it must be quite obvious that no one was acting sensibly. But can we admit that they were acting culturally? In the horrible moment of that beating everyone seemed to be united into thinking the action appropriate. What exactly had wired their brains to think this way? And you can bring all the nuance in the world to show that there are other stories (yes, there certainly are) or that you know other examples of people who weren't beaten (yes, sure, not everyone is beaten; this is true), or that the man who sells you red peas in Coronation Market in downtown Jamaica is obviously both gay and popular in his community (yes, yes, he probably is). But nuance of this kind is ultimately dishonest, not because it isn't true, but rather because it tries to suppress a much more urgent truth.

It was the same with some in my class. They wanted another truth – for Chinua Achebe to expand on the point that not all white people are racist. And if he had expanded on that, it most certainly would have been true. But not all truths are equal, and it is sad when nuance is co-opted so that some of us might get away with only facing the less important ones.

MAYBE BELLYWOMAN WAS ON "DI TAPE"
(2011)

Presented as the keynote address at University of Reading's "Shadows
and Shorelines Symposium: Literary Representations of Queer and
Postcolonial Mythical Beings"

Presentations of this kind often begin with a disclaimer of sorts,
so here is mine: the simple admission that though I'm not usually
nervous at podiums, I am today. It is, perhaps, the pressure of
the occasion, of giving this kind of a talk – a "keynote" address –
with the disturbing idea that I am about to set the tone, or deliver
a core message, or summarize the main points for today's
proceedings. And that this is an academic symposium makes it
all the more worrying for someone like me – a writer. While I
do move between the roles of academic and novelist, scholar and
poet, in moments like the present when I suspect that I may not
live up to the academic requirements of the occasion, when I am
about to speak about things I have more observed than researched,
I quickly pronounce myself as existing at just one end of this
admittedly false occupational binary. So that is my disclaimer: I
am an author, a poet, nothing more.

Today's symposium announces that it will look at "literary repre-
sentations of queer and postcolonial mythical beings". I apologize
that this essay does not actually consider any novels or poems, but
hopefully it will be received as a kind of "literary representation". In
calling this talk "Maybe Bellywoman was on di tape" I know I will
have to tell you who exactly Bellywoman is, but first I must tell you
about "di tape" and how it has become the mythical space I am
suggesting it has become.

Di Tape

If you had been in Jamaica some time after 2002, and you passed two men or two women on the road walking slowly to work, and you overheard a conversation – something perhaps about "the tape", they would probably have been referring to the famous (or infamous) "Don't draw mi tongue" speech given by Portia Simpson-Miller, Jamaica's then minister of Tourism – who would subsequently rise, and fall, then rise again to the position of prime minister. The expression "Don't draw mi tongue" is a threat. It imagines the tongue, dangerous, serpent-like, full of venom, but presently curled up, coiled in, inert, not troubling a soul. The colloquial expression translates: if you know what is best for you do not draw **out** my tongue, do not force me to reveal the very damning things that I could reveal about you.

Portia Simpson-Miller issued the warning in 2002 to an ambitious politician from the other side who had taken to the warpath attacking her. It was the usual: an election was looming so everything was fair-game. Finally, the ambitious politician accused Portia of some manner of fraud and this seemed to be the last straw. So one hot evening, in a subsequently much broadcast televised clip, Portia climbed onto her own podium, and while wagging her head from side to side and hitting her chest with evangelic enthusiasm, she sent a direct warning to her adversary. "Don't draw mi tongue" and then, intriguingly, "I have di tape. I have sent it to my lawyers."

Jamaica's rumour mills went into immediate production. What was on the tape? One of the most popular and scandalous rumours went like this – that the politician's girlfriend of the time was pregnant. Of course, it wasn't the allegation of breeding that was the scandal. If it had only been that, then the man would have been praised for his virility. Rather it was the supposed age of the bred. A mere teenager. And the tape that Portia alluded to, as the rumour went, had evidence of this. But all of this is unlikely. If you listen to Portia's speech it seems clear that she was alluding to some kind of evidence that exonerated her from the original accusations levelled against her. What is more likely is that those who either knew (or perhaps invented) the story of the politician's indiscretion wanted to give it wheels, and so this fortuitously intriguing and shadowy idea

about a "tape" became the vehicle. So from 2002 – 2006, this is what "di tape" was – mythical proof that one of Jamaica's politicians had committed carnal rape.

But in 2006, "di tape" came to mean something else altogether. Something more salacious and scandalous. And this now is "di tape" of which Beenie Man sings in his song "Bullet Proof", when he taunts his arch-nemesis Bounty Killer with: "Yu know Peter King dat's why a you one watch di tape, den have de nerve fi come chat up inna bad man face". This 2006 version is "di tape" that Kiprich sings of in his song "Show di tape", that Junior Reid sings of in his song "Di people dem caan wait, fi si who de pon de tape", and it is di tape of which DYCR makes mention when he chants:

> Leggo di tape, run di tape, buss di tape
> Wa yuh a hold on pon di tape fa
> I wonder if you deh pon it?

The singular tape in question here was in fact several tapes – maybe as many as thirty – taken from the home of Ambassador Peter King, murdered in Jamaica on 19th March 2006. Peter King, though married and with three children, was as publicly gay as one can be in Jamaica (you will notice I did not use the term "out" which I don't think, as a concept, maps particularly well onto a Jamaican situation). He was a man of society, a doyen, almost, in Jamaican business circles, in government circles and, yes, in gay circles as well. He was famous for the lavish parties he would hold for any of these groups. It was unfortunately – and perhaps inevitably – rumoured, too, that he had a predilection for street boys and used his power to invite them – vulnerable young men – into his house. A young man, Sheldon Pusey, was convicted of killing him.

But let us go back to the day of the murder and let me point out now a meta-videographic moment if you will, for as the news cameras showed footage of the crime scene – the police lifting out the body, the knife, and other bits of evidence – there it is. At least I'd like to imagine it is there: a tape of the tapes – dark video footage of what was supposed to contain even darker video footage.

Two weeks later, the local news website Yardflex.com explained what had already begun to happen with the tape in popular culture. Under the titillating headline, "Sex Tape Saga" it began:

R & B superstar R. Kelly had a highly incriminating one, and even
sexy socialite Paris Hilton had an energetic cameo in one… however
the 63 year-old former trade ambassador Peter King tops them all
with a whopping 30 sex tapes, each reportedly more lurid than the
next [sic].

Police sources were said to have revealed that the sex tapes, which
were in the hands of investigators, had "revealing" scenes involving
a number of well-known figures from the local media, business,
political and even the entertainment fraternities. The clout wielded
by these "pillars of society" set tongues wagging that the police were
a party to an extensive cover-up to save the reputations of these
individuals.

Betty Ann Blaine, convenor of Hear the Children's Cry, told
Yardflex.com, "There must be no cover-up, I know that the police
ha[ve] to take time to do a thorough investigation, and I am willing to
wait, as long as the truth will be told in the end."

In the meantime, the "Sex Tape Saga" graduated into an even
wider pop-cultural phenomenon, dominating water-cooler gossip,
where conversations were often punctuated by the provocative
question: *Yu nuh hear who and who de pon the tape?*

Concerning the first ("Portia") tape, I should point out that what
it generated was middle-class gossip – what in Jamaica we would call
"verandah chat", the kind of conversation that begins, "My darling,
have you heard the ghastly news…" One of my friends at the time,
a social scientist, without being elitist, insisted that this made it more
believable. In professorial mode he explained, "Middle class ru-
mours tend to be true. They're not changing the information; they're
just circulating it amongst themselves."

But the other tape was another kind of phenomenon altogether; it
was mythic both in size and texture, for it was a story that a
community could add to. There were, of course, no good intentions
in the way the story was being added to, and this constant querying
of who was on the tape and who wasn't meant that a wide range of
characters, from the Prime Minister to the quiet neighbour next
door, were constantly being written in or erased from this new
cultural text. And then calamity. What was just a worry in the Yardflex
article – the conspiracy theory that a cover up was being planned –
became true. The tapes disappeared. Gone. Vanished. Kaput.

And as we might imagine when this was announced, in churches all over the island the following Sunday, many a man found himself singing that old song with enthusiasm:

> Gone, gone, gone, gone
> Yes, my sins are gone …
> Buried in the deepest sea
> Yes that's good enough for me
> Never to be remembered anymore!

(Incidentally, if you want to know where to look for queer and postcolonial mythical beings, then look no further than a Jamaican church. There is something in the way that women sing lustfully to be possessed, ridden, filled up with the mythical being of God that has at times overtly sexual overtones – and all the more curious when men sing these songs with the same kind of ecstasy. Which is why I have always maintained that to conduct one of the more interesting studies on queer or gay Jamaican culture, one should go to church, and perhaps specifically, to the choir – but perhaps that kind of thing is so obvious, it would be like shooting crabs in a barrel.)

I think of myths as simply stories that have lost their authors, but the tapes became a myth because it was a story that had lost its evidence (quite literally for they had supposedly been kept in the evidence room of a jailhouse). The story then lost that which could tether it to the physical – to the actual. The tape became a myth, its footage became a mythical world, a mythical space – and the people who were on the tape became mythical beings.

Now once again I am shooting at crabs, but there is something to be said about this way of looking at queer or gay identities in postcolonial countries like Jamaica; they seem to live more comfortably in mythical rather than in actual spaces. I'm thinking here of figures like River Mumma – that great cock-tease, always trying to tempt men into her depths, but when it comes to it, absolutely impenetrable. Or I am thinking of figures like the orisha, Guede, that dandy of a man with his cigars, and famously bisexual. Or I am thinking of the trickster spider, Anansi, with his high-pitched voice, the ease with which he leaves his web in full drag – rouge and lipstick and his wife's high-heeled shows on all eight legs – off to con some

other animal out of a pot of food or money. All these queer, postcolonial, mythical beings might make us think of the mythical as a virtual closet, the place where our queerness can comfortably hide. And yet… and yet…

This is the problem, that this particularly western, first-world epistemology with its own ideas of closets and queerness and gayness – its attempt, yes, to describe traditionally victimized subjectivities, but with a language that, coming from the centre, will always wield its own power. It will always be a sort of colonial language, and a colonial language in which we try to translate other postcolonial experiences, perhaps not appreciating the long-standing axiom about translations, that in the process something is inevitably lost.

For me, the loss of the tapes allowed us to keep something: our imagination. The tape was supposed to do the opposite – to shut off imagination. It was to be final proof of gay activity in Jamaica. We wanted to see it – and there is something to be said for that, this curiosity which itself was erotic, a kind of national voyeurism. In the most base way, the most crass way, Jamaica wanted to see the homoerotic. We wanted to see two men, maybe more, hopefully naked, one inside the other. It would have been an unambiguous (and perhaps for many, disappointing) proof of the indigenously gay. Many Jamaicans have lived in a strange state of denial – insisting that homosexual behaviour and cultures are always foreign impositions. Homosexuality, according to this nationalist reading, has no place in Jamaica, in black cultures generally, in the African diaspora or in Africa itself. Such theories have been so thoroughly debunked by African historians that it isn't worth traversing that material now, but I am not unsympathetic to the reasons why black postcolonial nationalisms are so often constructed as being anti-homosexual. Consider the recent backlash in Jamaica because the British prime minister, David Cameron, has suggested that he will discontinue aid to countries that refuse to repeal their buggery laws. Jamaica has reacted quite badly to this kind of imposition. How dare a foreign culture dictate what we should and shouldn't do? Jamaicans are asking if David Cameron, and Britain generally, has no respect for our own Jamaican laws. We understand that we are being seen as barbarians. We resent this, of course, and we resent being given lectures on Human Rights by people who for centuries never re-

garded us as human at all. But there is no hint of irony in this protest; nowhere does it seem to dawn on Jamaicans that the laws we are now holding on to are not Jamaican but British, that these laws and moralities were imposed on us a long time ago, and they are in fact part of our colonial inheritance. In all fairness, this fact does not seem to dawn on David Cameron either – that the savage barbarism he would like to rescue us from is exactly the one his country gave us.

But "homosexuality" (and I must put that term between quotation marks) did exist in Africa and I have a sense of indigenous cultures being able to accommodate transgressive gender and sexual performances, but known *in* their own terms and *on* their own terms. Such performances and the processes by which they have been accommodated do not map easily onto neo-colonial notions or cultures of "queer" or "LGBT". They do not necessarily live under the banner of "homosexuality" etc. However, in Jamaica, we live in a neo-colonial world where words and concepts are being imported all the time – and far fewer of our own words and concepts are being exported. So the postcolonial subject begins to understand himself in the imported terms, through someone else's pitying gaze, and understands himself as oppressed. He wouldn't be wrong either. I just think it is all very complex.

I want to tell you now about how some of the things that in this British academic context you might call "queer", we in Jamaica would call something else – or call several different things, depending on the context. We might even call it "the movement of the Bellywoman".

I admit, by the way, that I will be talking about beings that are more real than they are mythical, but perhaps exist on the border – the folk getting ready to transition into folklore.

<p style="text-align:center">★</p>

I went to my first nine-night in Jamaica maybe eleven or twelve years ago. There was a cleaning woman who worked at the University (I believe she still works there) – Miss Patsy – and her mother had died. Miss Patsy's mother was from St Thomas, and in Jamaica St Thomas is supposed to be the parish where you will still see Rolling Calf, or River Mumma, or Old Higue.

It is a place where you might still see frogs with padlocks pushed through their mouths, where you will still find the obeah man, and the myal-man, and the modder-woman. If there are any mythical beings left in Jamaica, their address is somewhere in St Thomas. So the St Thomas community was going to see Miss Patsy's mother off in the old way. It was going to be a traditional deadyard with Kumina drums, with the slaughtering of white hens, and the throwing of rum. This is why I went – because I wanted to see this world and this culture which, as a boy from the city, I had not been much exposed to.

The directions to the deadyard were confusing and the journey itself an adventure. It was night of course and at last we came to a road without streetlights. We felt certain were in the right place, and simultaneously lost. Nothing was on the road. Finally our headlights illuminated a lone man walking by himself. We drove up and asked if we were where we should be. He told us, yes, we were there – that we should just park a hundred yards or so up ahead, listen for the drums and part the bushes and walk into the hills. If we did that, we would come to the deadyard.

Well, we got there. Miss Patsy came out from hiding, only briefly, to say hello to us and to thank us for coming. Then she went back into hiding. She had seen Kumina before, seen the ways people became possessed, and didn't want any part of it. Kumina is a moment when real people invite other beings into them, spirits to ride them. This is what I mean by people existing on a border, moving into their mythical selves, stepping out of folk and into folklore. Miss Patsy hid, but we on the other hand, as pseudo-ethnographers, wanted to see it all. The Kumina drums began to beat, that incredibly infectious horse-galloping rhythm, and it wasn't long before people had gotten into the kind of frenzy that Miss Patsy feared. It was as wonderful as I thought it would be, and I remember one man in particular, possessed, dancing an incredible dance, and everyone being moved by it. We gave him space even as the dance seemed to take him further and further away from himself, even to a dangerous place. And observing him more closely, I remember thinking there was some-thing strangely curious about this man. I wouldn't have thought the word "queer" immediately, nor, as I would say these days, was there a kind of "gaydar" going off in my head. I would probably think that

now, but that's not really the point. As his dance continued as if to a place he would never come back from, another man finally seized him from behind, not to stop him exactly, but just to hold him back. So these two men were now dancing together, their bodies pressed against each other, both of them groaning to the Kumina drums, men on the border of myth, holding on to each other's bodies. They danced together for quite some time, such intimacy, their hands occasionally reaching for each other's face. Never before in Jamaica had I seen something so tender, so erotic, and so public happen between two men. And of course it made me think about this thing that could happen in the shadowy space of Kumina, without so much as a flinch or a worry from anyone else, that couldn't happen elsewhere. It is no wonder that people sometimes feel that queer lives hardly exist in Jamaica, or that they have no agency (which of course is true in its own way as well), when, in order to see these things you have to park your car on a lonely road, part the bushes and march into the hillside in search of drums, and dissolve yourself into silhouettes.

To see a mythical being in Jamaica requires creativity, odd rituals, a stretching of the neck if not of the mind. Sometimes, they say, you must spread your legs, bend over completely, and look between your legs. Or else you must take the matter from a dog's eyes and rub it into your own. Then you might see a duppy at his own funeral, sitting quietly on the coffin. Or you might see River Mumma sitting on a rock in the middle of a river. Sometimes, in order to see the kind of being which in this British context you might call "queer", but which in Jamaica we might call something else, requires similar creativity. That is why I am glad that the videographic evidence was lost, subsumed back into the shadows, because now these queer Caribbean beings will not be served up to us so easily on either plate or tape. They require from us something greater: an elastic imagination.

Come now and see Bellywoman, for I am not unaware that I have gotten quite far into this essay, perhaps even progressing towards its end, and my title character has not yet made his first appearance, although he may have been lurking in the shadows of each sentence, on the shorelines of my paragraphs.

We are still in St Thomas, and the season is there as it is here, late November going into the Christmas season, maybe a few years ago. The bouncy music that you are hearing consists of fifes and fiddles

and rusty graters that are no longer being used to grate coconuts or sweet potatoes. All this light-hearted racket is for one of the few remaining Jonkanoo bands getting ready to march. This sort of thing used to be very common in Jamaica, but it isn't any more. If you want to find such things today, however, as you know, you will find it in St Thomas.

Jonkanoo is a word of disputed etymology. Some say it is Malinke, where jonkanoo would translate to "the sound of the slaves". Others say it is a festival named after a mythical slave called "John Canoe", who perhaps, if we are the take his last name as a sign, sailed all the way back to Africa. Others root it in other West African tribes and celebrations, but no one knows for sure. The celebration happens in Jamaica, and definitely in the Bahamas, and maybe in Belize as well. It is a parade featuring a strange and nightmarish cast of characters, from the skeletal Hobby Horse, to the Pitchy Patchy figure in all its rags from the Great House (yes, a character with the actual effigy of a house on his head), to the Policeman with his baton, and the Devil with his fork. And finally – here he is – Bellywoman – with a ridiculously sized ass, and a ridiculously sized belly in front. These two things jiggle the more that Bellywoman dances. And what makes this performance all the more ridiculous/odd/queer is that Bellywoman is always played by a man.

Jonkanoo isn't a religious festival of any kind. There is nothing sacred here. The characters represent a kind of secular excess. They chase the children and scare them. Bellywoman, however, provides some comic relief – but do not take him for granted – he can scare as well as the worst of them – this bearded woman, this pregnant man, this impossible being. The Jamaica Cultural Development Commission has recently been trying to revive Jonkanoo, to prevent it completely dying out, and by now I have seen a few of these bands. I have seen a few Bellywomen. And always, always, I find myself thinking – there is something curious about the man playing this role, though I don't think the word "queer" nor, again, am I immediately aware of some kind of "gaydar" going off. It is simply of interest to me the ways in which Jamaican culture makes space for transgendered performances, but always in these almost mythical characters.

But as if Bellywoman really was pregnant, this performance of

woman by man in turn begets a long line of drag performances in Jamaican folk culture, a genealogy, as it were, of island cross-dressers – from what we call "roots theatre" straight (pun intended) to the ghettos and the killing fields of Jamaica's inner cities. Last year I wrote a facetious note on Facebook which, to my initial concern, was picked up the next morning by the *New York Times* and later by the *Los Angeles Times*. It had to do with the capture of the Jamaican drug lord, Dudus, who had been hiding from both Jamaican and American police for months. The final capture of Dudus saw him, humiliatingly, in a wig and this made me reflect on the long line of bandits from our stridently heteronormative island who were not above wearing a bit of drag. Before Dudus there was Natty Morgan, the most dangerous murderer in Jamaica at the time, who had escaped from jail and eluded authorities for months and who, it was well known, had a great arsenal of both guns and women's clothes to help him escape difficult situations. And again, before they actually captured Dudus, a near civil war broke out in Jamaica to defend him. He had supposedly barricaded himself in the community of Tivoli Gardens where his supporters armed themselves to the teeth ready for a fight. You must understand that the community had done this before and had basically won, so there was precedence. On the day that the police and army finally went in (provoked by the impatient community that had finally burnt down two nearby police stations), seventy-two men were eventually killed; several of them, it is reported, died wearing dresses. And I imagine them – author that I am – this tribe of bellywomen, with comically large asses and pregnant bellies, holding on to the hems of their frocks with one hand, and their uzi guns with the other, and with almost balletic grace running and shooting and dodging bullets, at least for a little while. And I wish that something like this was on di tape.[1]

Di tape – and we are back now to Peter King – was lost. But I would like to imagine (and indeed its loss allows me to imagine…) that there was more on it than just men rogering the be-jesus out of each other. I would like to imagine that on it was some of the complexity of being, and of queer beings, in a postcolonial country like Jamaica.

And so I would like to imagine that maybe Legba was on the tape – just for a brief cameo – this god who guards the crossroads, who in

Haiti is called Guede, with his top hat and suit, this dandy of a god-man, blowing out billows of cigar smoke.

Or else I would like to imagine that Anansi was on di tape, in mascara, with his high-pitched nasal twang, laughing at some joke or the other. And if we, in Jamaica, had seen him on di tape, it would have stopped us dead to see this most sacred being, our most sacred selves in such a space. We could no longer whisper at the cooler, "You know who and who deh pon di tape?" for suddenly that who and who would include our gods, and therefore would include us.

And maybe there were whole choirs on di tape, and choir leaders, deacons and church pastors. Maybe there were Maroons on di tape. And a binghi man. And a myal man.

And maybe there were moments of Kumina on di tape. That the darkness on the tape was not only that of bedrooms with closed windows and doors, but the actual darkness of night, of bushes in St Thomas, and the strange ceremonies that happen there, the men who become possessed and dance both away and towards themselves, with no reproach, indeed with utter respect from those who stand off to the side and watch them.

Maybe one of our national heroes was on di tape – someone like Bustamante, even. I thought about Alexander Bustamante a lot for my PhD because I was interested in his letters to *The Gleaner* when he returned to Jamaica at the age of fifty, after a thirty year absence. In the letters, this famously flamboyant dandy of a man, reinvents himself, and writes an utterly fabricated past. According to his letters he had fought in the Spanish civil war and had degrees in Portuguese, Italian and Spanish. But these are all lies. And that this man, who didn't father any of his own children but became father of the nation – this man who finally got married at the age of eighty, more in need of a caregiver than a lover, that he insisted on leaving his adventures between the ages of twenty and fifty in the shadows, seems a very curious thing to me, very odd, very queer, something ripe for rereading.

And maybe Bellywoman was on di tape, that wonderfully impossible being, and all that he gives birth to – a whole tribe of queer, postcolonial, mythical beings.

End Note

1. It seems now in Jamaica there is emerging a third incarnation of "di tape". A *New York Times* article in December, 2011 revealed that there was actually an American plane taking aerial footage of the insurrection in Tivoli Gardens. Calls have now come for the Jamaican government to get a hold of that tape.

AN INTERVIEW – COMPOSED OF THINGS ASKED, AND THINGS SAID, AND THINGS THAT WERE NEVER SAID BUT MAYBE SHOULD HAVE BEEN.
(2008)

Some interviews – like dates – go bad from the beginning. It could be a simple case of "no chemistry", or even worse, a case of "spirit don't tek", as we say in the Caribbean. What follows is one such interview. It went bad from the beginning.

I had not met Gloria when she first contacted me over the Christmas period of 2008; I still have not met her. The world however is so small that I imagine we will eventually do so. It will be at a conference on something like "The poetry of the African Diaspora", and when she sees me she will probably fix me with a devastating cut-eye.

Having established contact a few weeks earlier, in early 2009 Gloria emailed me a series of questions. I had agreed to be inter-viewed for a journal whose focus was on African poetry. Though at the time I had never been to Africa, I imagined such a journal embraced the African diaspora as well – black communities around the world. But perhaps this was part of the unacknowledged prob-lems and tensions in the interview – a reductive idea of what black poetry should be about and how it should be written. It was as if, in Gloria's mind, I was writing down the wrong vision.

Gloria was based in Nigeria; the second interviewer, Irene, was based in Canada, while I was in Scotland – a real global spread. For obvious and practical reasons, the interview took place over emails.

Gloria confessed in her first email, "I love your poems." But she had only read my first book, *Kingdom of Empty Bellies*. It seemed odd to me to conduct an interview only based on that book. My creative headspace was no longer there. I arranged for her to get the second, and I suspect her opinion changed once she had read it. She was no

longer a fan – neither of my work nor of my subsequent answers. This should not have been a bad thing, necessarily. Too often writers are interviewed by their fans, the questions soft and hardly challenging. Gloria will not be accused of posing soft questions. Quite the contrary, they became increasingly aggressive – even offensive. On my part, I grew increasingly annoyed – whether justifiably or not, you the present reader, can be the judge. Irene, the good cop, tried valiantly to keep the peace, but her efforts were in vain.

Perhaps this rather long interview is not one that should ever be published. Gloria and Irene certainly chose not to. They probably chalked it up as a bad experience with a needlessly cantankerous and immature Caribbean writer. And yet I think, even in the annoyance of it all, I began to articulate things that I still believe.

<p style="text-align:center">★ ★ ★</p>

Gloria: Tell me about yourself.

> [This seemed a strangely vague way to start an interview. I didn't know how to answer such a broad question. I confess however that it is a question that has always annoyed me – no fault to the interviewer – and so maybe it was my honest answer that started our interview on a wrong foot.]

Kei: "Tell me about yourself" is one of those questions I have a particular aversion to, simply because the range of answers seems so impossibly broad that I am always rendered immediately silent. What exactly do you want to know, Gloria? What are my hobbies, biographical information, ambitions, eccentricities, preoccupations? I'll be better at answering questions a bit more specific.

Gloria: We are interested in some biographical information of your good self. Some of us who have seen your books will *surely* like to start from there.

> [I thought "some of those who have seen my books" would have *surely* read the back cover to get a clue of my biography. But I obliged.]

Kei: Well I was born in Jamaica thirty years ago, and I grew up
 in one of those boring suburbs on the outskirts of Kingston.
 I lived there – in Jamaica, and in that particular suburb, until
 last year. There was a year when I went away to school in
 England. But for the most part I have lived in Jamaica. Now
 I teach at the University of Glasgow, so this now is my second
 year away from home.

Irene: The figure of the woman is often present in your poetry,
 more present than the male figure, and her character comes
 across as much more positive than the men that you mention.
 Why is that? Does it have anything to do with your own
 experience with women back in Jamaica? Have they been positive
 role models for you, more positive than the men you have
 dealt with?

 [I thought this question was fair… well, until it began to prompt
 for a certain kind of response at the end. I realize I didn't like
 the impulse behind this – the need to search tediously for
 some autobiographical justification behind the poems and also
 to have the author validate the critic's own political
 interpretations. To put it plainly, it seemed to me that I was
 being invited to engage in a sort of male bashing, but I still
 hope I was gracious enough.]

Kei: People keep on mentioning this, so they must be right, but
 I'm not completely sure why that is – this privileging of the
 female subject. There isn't any agenda at work, none that I
 am conscious of, and I'd also be hesitant to root it in my own
 experience of women (as opposed to men) in Jamaica. I'll hazard
 a guess though, and say it has a lot to do with my experience
 of reading. I guess, as a writer, I've come after the explosion
 of female writers of the 1980s – I grew up reading Lorna
 Goodison and Olive Senior and Erna Brodber from the
 Caribbean, and Gloria Naylor and Toni Morrison from America,
 all these women who themselves were writing about women.
 So women were very present and very large in my fictional
 landscape. I've simply ended up writing the kinds of stories I
 liked reading, and they are inhabited by the kinds of characters
 I fell in love with.

Gloria: Still on your preoccupation with womanhood and feminine
activities – recipes, religion, onions, passivity, love and, most
importantly, the passion of your poetry, all these seem in
agreement with French feminists who would insist that there
is distinctly a special language and mode of images mostly
employed by the female gender. Although in the *Empty Bellies*
blurb commentary Lorna Goodison referred to you as "he",
how apt is the guess that you are a female (an important omission
in your introduction) or (please don't think this rude) gay?

[I wonder why is it that when people do in fact mean to be
rude that they put in this disclaimer, "Please don't think this
rude"? It is a bit like when people say, "I don't mean to be
racist, but..." Nothing good ever comes from these
"disclamatory" beginnings.

 I suspect that what Gloria really meant to say was, "Look, I read
your first book of poetry and I liked it well enough. I liked it
because it was full of strong black women, and I am comfortable
celebrating that figure. I am a strong black woman myself. But I
do not care for your second book because it deals with wimps,
effeminate men, a lack of masculinity. Forgive me, but none of
this seems particularly 'African'."]

Kei: Was it really an "important" omission? Maybe it's different
where you're from, but I can't imagine someone casually
declaring their genders when introducing themselves: Hello,
I am Gloria and I am a woman; Hello, I am Kei and I have a
penis. I really tend to assume such things are obvious. Now,
it doesn't mean my assumption is correct, especially in the
present format over emails and with an androgynous name
like "Kei", but that is what I assume nonetheless. I must say,
and I don't care what theoretical school you want to tie the
suggestion to, it seems to me spectacularly reductive (and even
offensive) to suggest that a female sensibility can only be written
by women or gay men. Was Faulkner, was Hardy, was Fielding,
was Achebe, was Earl Lovelace drawing on some gay gene when
they wrote about women? Must a woman be a butch lesbian
to write about men?

[Her next question was much more civil. I don't imagine this is because she felt like being more civil, but it was the format of the interview, in which I got a few questions simultaneously.]

Gloria: Sound of words, rhythm and musical excerpts overflow in your poems. What do you surmise as the relationship between music and poetry? And is "Dance" a recurrent motif in your poetry, an icon for self expression or symbolism for individual freedom from societal (human and non human) constrictions?

Kei: I suppose I think poetry at its best is always a kind of music. I tell my students to ask of every poem they write – where is the surprise and where is the music? These two things are integral for me. As for dance, yes it is a recurrent motif – but I'm saying that as an objective fact. I'm looking now over the work and I see that dance has come up a whole lot; I'm almost surprised. The point is there is no agenda there again, but it is all of what you say it is.

[When I said that phrase "it is all of what you say it is" I was probably already becoming annoyed at the language of the interview – how it gracelessly and awkwardly drew from a certain academic register, trying to attach itself to all kinds of literary theories, but often slipping into malapropisms. Maybe there is a place for this kind of language, but an interview of this nature didn't seem to be one of them. I cruelly guessed that she was only trying (and failing) to advertise her own intelligence. My annoyance at this would explode later.]

Gloria: Although your poetry promises a combination of art and skills, however, one may wonder at the general sterility and futility reflected through reinforced images of fragmentation, a landscape of emptiness, poverty and want, a blight in religion, etched-deep feelings of separation, nostalgia, and serial losses – all Naipaulian notions of existentialist pessimism. Are these really true reflections of modern Caribbean society?

Kei: But of course [these reflections] are true. At least, they are my truths, as I see them. And these kinds of reflections were never peculiar to Naipaul. I think our problem with Naipaul has been, as you say it, that there is such a deep pessimism

and also a meanness in how he sees the land and its people. But not many Caribbean people have ever denied that there is a "truth" in what he is saying. Many of us merely feel it is often a one-sided or exaggerated truth. The Caribbean is a place I am very much in love with. It is home after all. But this does not mean it is above critique, and I can only hope the two things are present in my work, both the love and the critique.

Gloria: One may expect that the "love" might have been expressed "straight" like the negative "truths" you spoke of, probably in construct with the idea of "realism" which finds expression in the late 20th and early 21st centuries, and the present practice of art as by product of fracture, loss and neurosis. In most poetry, especially of contemporary African, American or British expression, you find it all there. Perhaps I cherish the type of positive idealism that has been said of Whitman, Che and few traditional poetry [sic] of positive affirmation and inspiration (not one of losses, regrets and nostalgia). But then it appears we are caught on to the era of "Self" as opposed to "Communal" and most things about self must be infused with serial reversals to attract the kind of attention the West rivets upon art.

[What she meant to say was, "Your poetry has become too white – confessional, clever. Myself, I prefer the more obvious kinds of revolutionary chanting."]

Kei: You say things like "One may expect" and "Perhaps I cherish…" and "But then it appears" which all seem to me like you're declaring your own subjectivity, and that my own poetry, as you read it, falls a bit outside of that – of what you "expect or cherish". I think we all do this – we all draw our own small circles of what we consider worthwhile poetry to be, and maybe it's unfortunate for me that my poems cannot fall in the centre of every circle. I have to respect that people look for different things in art, and I wouldn't want to try and convince you today that what I'm doing, and how I see my own art, is the right way. Now while you're trying to imply the opposite, I can assure you I have never sat down and calculatedly thought out what kind of poetry might appeal to the Western World

(which I am, incidentally, very much a part of) and then set
out to write those poems. There is too little financial reward
in poetry to spend so much energy. I think most of us simply
write the poems we are passionate about, and we hope they
pick up a few readers.

Gloria: William Summer surmises that "human society tries hard
to adapt itself to any condition in which it finds itself… the
way the foot adapts itself to an ill-made boot." However some
African historians would have us believe that this attitude of
docile acceptance is most peculiar to the black race. Ironically
your insistence on fragmentation ("we are bruised into
ourselves") as a norm which is replicated in "asphalt and gravel",
your concept of beingness ("Broken"), echoes a certain fatalism
of adaptive docility. Is this is your own attitude to contemporary
Caribbean history and politics?

Kei: When, in "The Broken" the poem says "we are bruised into
ourselves", it isn't merely speaking on behalf of Caribbean
people, or black people. It is reaching out much further than
that and trying to understand a fundamental part of our humanity.
Perhaps you see "fragmentation", or "brokenness" as I put it
in the poem, as a bad thing. I don't. I think it is exactly what
connects all of us – that in some way, in some place, each of
us carry around different hurts and insecurities and profoundly
deep longings, and it is these things that make us human, that
make us our most honest and noble and beautiful selves.

Gloria: Your opinion about our human connectivity is valid, though
not everyone would situate it within the locus of "hurts",
"insecurities" and "profoundly deep longings" as you have done.
There is a concept of "wholeness" as the connectivity of all
beings in a universal spiritual sense. It has been found all through
Egyptology, Classical Greek ontology, and American
transcendentalism of the 19th century. Do you think that this
awareness is almost lost on writers from the Caribbean?

Kei: I can't speak on behalf of the whole Caribbean. "We" are too
many countries and too many languages. My voice hasn't yet
achieved that level of plurality, nor has my tongue split into so
many pieces. I am, incidentally, similarly suspicious whenever
I hear people pretend to speak on behalf of all of Africa.

So then, to speak personally – you're right: the concept of wholeness does bore me and strikes me as inevitably false. I could be wrong, but "wholeness" always seems to me like a veneer which we are very caught up in defending and articulating and reaching for – but is it ever achieved, and if it is achieved does it stay that way for very long? I don't think so. I'm much more attracted to vulnerability in people and in art.

Irene: When reading the first poems of *There is An Anger that Moves* one of the sentiments that jumps to mind (and heart) right away is the hurt and anger that the poetic subject still feels towards the colonial agent, either because he is thinking retrospectively (immersed in history) or because he encounters in England remnants of that arrogant colonial "personae" that mock his "difference" and his way of speaking. This anger and hurt have been "sung" beautifully by many Caribbean and African poets. Do you see yourself as a follower of that line of poetry, the poetry that is intended to explore the woes related to colonialism still so present in the psyche of black colonized peoples? How would you say that your poetry differs from those who have gone before you? And who, would you say, amongst those poets, has influenced your poetry the most?

[I was sad that the "good cop" was asking this. It again seemed a desperate attempt to make me into a suitable "black poet". Maybe I should have just said it then; I should have declared my hand with apologies: Look, (I should have said) I'm sorry I cannot be your angry black poet; I'm actually angry about a lot of shit, but maybe they're not the things you're angry about; I'm sorry I cannot be bothered to fight the battles that I always assumed had already been won on my behalf; I'm sorry that I'm comfortable in my own black skin. And it's not that I don't realize that this very comfort isn't problematic at times, and that it implicates and accuses me on other levels of class and privilege, but I'm working that out for myself.]

Kei: When *There is An Anger That Moves* came out I was fascinated by what two reviewers said – that despite the title there was surprisingly not much "anger" in it. That's my own feeling

actually, which I'm not proposing is necessarily the truth. The text, of course, is there to suggest however many number of readings to however many number of readers. But there you have it – I myself don't see much anger in it. There is of course the very first poem which you alluded to, which perhaps is undeniably "angry". It was interesting writing that poem because in that sequence I was trying to write a number of emotions and positions that the migrant might feel and I was conscious of myself exaggerating my way into feelings I'd never actually had, or not to that extent. Perhaps most of my poems swell with some kind of passion, but again I'm not sure that passion is usually "anger".

I'm sorry but I certainly do not see myself as a follower of the line of poetry you describe. I would be affecting something that I didn't truly feel, and I don't want to take up an agenda that has been written down already and bequeathed to me. You know, I think as poets we must be cautious not only of clichés of language, but also clichés of self.

Gloria: Then why anger as a title if you are truly not a follower of that line of poetry? Many would oppose the notion as escapist that once a theme has been written down already you have no need of them even where there are such valid nuances in your discourse. Because the tendency is that a discourse is continued by succeeding generations directly or indirectly and thus the colonial/post colonial experience is an inescapable fact of Caribbean literature as it is of Caribbean political life. Or is the fact of art as writing and talking back a luxury that the Caribbean writer can ill afford in his wonted individualism and preoccupation with self?

Kei: Why the title? Because it made sense to me. It was either that or "The Broken". The line "there is an anger that moves" is one that recurs in a couple of the poems. So there is resonance there. And I like how it suggests a kind of red-hot passion that moves us – and by movement I mean something both emotional and spatial – a passion that makes us move our feet in dance for instance, or scream. As I said, I want my poetry, in the end, to be full of that – a "moving" passion. Now I wouldn't have called the collection "Angry!" because it isn't

making that kind of declaration and I do not write that kind of poetry. But *There Is Anger That Moves* is a different title altogether, don't you think?

Now, to the other part of your question; I used to say that I had an advantage, that coming a couple generations after Derek Walcott and Kamau Brathwaite, I didn't have to choose between Walcott's poetry of the self, or Brathwaite's poetry of the community. My poems take on a range of voices and perspectives. But I no longer even agree with this dialogic relationship. It seems to me that a poetry of the self is also a poetry about the community, because that is where the self exists. You're right that we must avoid navel gazing, the kind of preoccupation with ourselves that would interest no one else, but only bad poets do that kind of foolishness! When Walcott, for instance, writes a poetry that is largely autobiographical, that is drawing on his own vision and experience, he is inevitably also writing about the community in which the "self" finds itself.

[What I should have also said was: It is time to re-conceive this notion of the centre. The centre for me is no longer Britain. I live in Britain and for me that means I live on the periphery. Isn't that essentially what a diaspora is – a group of people that have dispersed from the centre? The centre for me is now the Caribbean. If I am writing back to anyone that is who I am writing back to.]

Gloria: Talking of "clichés of language and self" brings to mind disputations over concepts of "originality" and "influences" in art which scholars have used to explain the similar moods, themes, and manners of expression found in the various arts of the world. Wouldn't you agree in this sense that there is actually nothing "original" in poetry and, indeed, all creative art, as these ideas have been expressed at some time and somewhere by someone else before or in our time. Classical "zeitgeist" and Jungian theories of a "collective unconscious" have attempted to account for this condition but many writers usually don't take kindly to the idea of their work not being original. As Irene mentions

here, how far can we claim to be original in using materials and ideas that surround us all the time?

Kei: Wow... each of your questions come with a few hefty pounds of one theory or another attached to its poor little feet, as if to give that question more body – but maybe I'm not as well read as you think and this language you're talking is simply one I don't speak or think in; so forgive me because I am getting a little lost in some of the scholarly acrobatics. But I'll forge ahead and try my best to answer what I think it is you might be asking. I've found that the rhetoric which declares "everything has been said already, it's all clichés in a sense" is most often spouted by the less than talented poet who has begun to suspect his own limitation. In a last ditch attempt he invents this sermon that exonerates his failures. But I have no time for that. I do believe wholly in the originality of art. It is perhaps as you say, quite difficult to have a new idea. But an idea isn't a poem. Language is. And it really is not that hard to say something in a way in which it has, in fact, never been said before. I state that categorically. In this sense, originality is quite easy – and one would have to be lazy, I think, to forego being original with language. Strangely enough, I think originality is one of the very basic things an artist must learn to do – because once you realize it is quite easy to be "original", you then realize that being original is not the same as being good. If we imagine "excellent art" as a ladder that one is climbing, then originality would be one of the very low rungs; we conquer that task very quickly, and then face bigger challenges.

Irene: The other very strong sentiment that comes to mind (and soul and body...) ...

[Irene had clearly meditated and connected with her Zen before this interview. I liked this about her.]

Irene: when reading your poetry, and especially *Kingdom of Empty Bellies*, is the trauma, the madness and the psychic fragmentation that resulted from the transatlantic slave trade. This condition of *sickness*, often manifests itself in an exacerbated (phobic) fear of water, of waves, of dark catacomb and coffin-like places

(e.g., "Granna's Eyes", "Aquaphobia", "Noctiphobia"). There is also the idea that the resolution of that *sickness* entails the facing up of certain fears, the direct encounter with that same water or the entrance in those dark claustrophobic places by learning how to swim for instance. Sometimes water, sea, and the blue eyes of Grandma all seem to merge in one single substance, a liquid and fluid substance that becomes the vehicle (the *way*) that permits a symbolical voyage to the ancestral land of Africa. We get the impression that such a voyage offers great solace allowing the faraway land and the faraway past to enter the *mourning sick person* [sic] and in that process a sense of relief and catharsis is attained even if only momentarily. Here I see a similarity between you and the St Lucian poet Derek Walcott. And I am thinking of his verse "I have no nation now but the imagination." Can you elaborate on these subjects?

Kei: It's odd, I haven't thought about the poem "Granna's Eyes" in quite some time, and I think that's because I've tried to forget it. It's the poem that embarrasses me most in that first collection.

[In retrospect, I do not think I should have started like that. Irene had given the poem a very gracious and generous reading, and my response was to dismiss its artistic merit. This now seems to me a rather mean-spirited thing to do and I wish I could take it back.]

Kei: [The poem] went through several lives – first as a short story, then as a poem, then back to a short story, then a different kind of a poem, and I'm not sure it ever truly found its perfect shape.

All of what you say about it is true, but I think I was trying to say something else too. The trauma is there, but the trauma in a strange way becomes beautiful and magical. I mean think of it: the whole ocean existing in this woman's eyes – enough water to flood her house and village – it is kind of fantastic. But in the end, it is something she has to let go of; she is holding on to pain simply for the sake of holding on to it, and this thing can become addictive if we let it. This is perhaps

why I don't want to lock myself in the tradition of protest poetry – or at least my own understanding of that tradition – because it often holds on to pain and anger and a righteous kind of passion simply for the sake of holding on to it.

Irene: Yes I agree with your last remarks here for even though the poem is pointing to the trauma and suffering that resulted from slavery, it is also telling us one must see oneself as more than what the past made of us, one must see oneself as capable of putting that past aside and start a new life, a life that does not fall into fatalistic victimization and passiveness. There seems to be the idea that if one continuously blames the colonizers and the slave traders for all one's sorrows one gets stuck in an unproductive impasse and is thus prevented from taking positive steps and even responsibility for one's own life. I actually think that some of your poems, in both collections, seem to point to the power of individual responsibility by attempting to exit the collective wounded Caribbean psychic, or by pointing to the sterility that can come from focusing on it too much. Could you comment on this idea further?

Kei: I suppose it a warning I'm often giving myself. You see – I recognize in my own person certain tendencies – an ability, a propensity, to get worked up about any number of issues. But sometimes this thing can become a drug. When we're filled with moral outrage, in a way I think, quite subtly, we begin to affirm our own goodness, our own righteousness – and that really can become addictive. So I become suspicious of myself when I linger too long in this wounded place, in the place of the victim, because I think in a way we become much more committed to the battle than to its victory; in a way we no longer want to win, because that would be the end of our "fix".

Irene: The Grandmother often transmutes, I would even say, into the African continent, she is the "womb" that was stolen from the slaves brought to the Americas, the thing that one misses and yearns for, the thing that perhaps can give us solace by "placing" us back in that *lieu* where we came from, that locale that we perceive as *really ours*, for this place, this new world still feels strange and not ours. The Grandmother, in her oldness,

and in the ceremonies that she performs becomes the African continent itself, that thing that one can only imagine and reconstruct mentally through fragments and stories that we may have heard from older family members who serve as messengers of the remote... Yet, she also becomes the agent that can resolve (or come to terms with) the identity struggle of the descendant of the slave and the trauma associated with it, as the ending of the poem "Granny's Eyes" seems to indicate: "her feet planted on two waves/like Jesus./There is a time to drown/and a time to walk on water./The ocean too has its end" (p. 42). She is even Jesus, a powerful divine entity that can heal the wounds of the present by connecting the continents and making a home in the New World, an entity that travels through time and space and somehow makes the "here and now" have sense and be "whole". How do you agree to this interpretation?

[What I should have said was, "Jeewhiz that's a rather long question!" But how could I say that? It was my own fault, because at the beginning I told them to be more specific. Still, I was intrigued by these questions that were really larger thesis statements that simply wanted me to affix a stamp at the end.]

Kei: Well, it sounds like a fascinating interpretation, and yes I can see where the text is probably saying something quite close to that. It's just that I'm not consciously an Africanist or Pan-Africanist, whatever those terms might mean now – I'm not even sure. My personal politics don't revolve around those particular longings. Of course I grew up in a country of largely black, African-Caribbean people and our imagination of Africa was important to us and our sense of self – so yes, that's there in the poems.

Gloria: Your resistance to all "labels", and categorization echoes the attitudes of many writers among us. Irene here, in 2008 Literary Chat, is a good example. Yet we are in a world that believes in labels and taxonomy as signposts to "meaning" and understanding in human communication. Fundamentally, humans rely on earlier knowledge to make new meanings and is this not similar to what poets, writers and scholars, including yourself, do?

Kei: In fact I do not resist "all labels" as you say. For example, I
don't resist the label "Caribbean". And I would not as strongly
resist the label "narrative poetry" as opposed to "protest poetry"
as a description of the poetic tradition I'm working in. I don't
even have a great problem with the label "queer". But you
see, what a certain kind of academic does, and does really well
– sometimes quite eloquently – is to take each text as a soapbox
onto which he or she climbs and begins spouting his or her
own politics, sometimes without seeming to care what the
text is far more likely to be saying. So the labels I resist are
the labels that are imposed on me which I frankly don't care
for, which don't seem to fit.

Let me explain why I resist the label "protest poetry" for
instance: it is because I generally find such poems dull, juvenile,
full of unearned and lofty sentiments, and having too little
regard for language, sound, rhythm etc. Is this true for all protest
poetry? Clearly it isn't. And what's more I don't have a problem
with "protest" or any declaration happening in my poems. I
do it all the time. What I'm resisting is the particular TRADITION
of protest poetry and it is a simple recognition on my part
that this is not what motivates my work.

Irene: There is in your poetry a very powerful spiritual dimension
captured beautifully by your playful and dynamic language
which has the capacity to make the reader feel the levitation
of the character that you are describing. This spiritual dimension
is often visible in the figure of the woman, or put forward
through the behaviour of women who go to church frequently
– an older woman, an aunt, a mother or a grandmother... I
especially enjoy those poems for we experience with them a
rising above the sorrows of the here and now and attain a larger
personhood as I would call it, with the self becoming merged
with the greater "I". Is this trait linked to a certain epistemology
and ontology which would differ from what some may call a
more rational and material western perspective? We are also
able to see how material poverty and suffering often transmutes
into these ecstatic spiritual dimensions as if the women
experiencing "the kingdom of empty bellies" have no choice
but to rise above it and find solace in spirituality. Sometimes,

the singing of the women in church becomes an actual call, a call to a God that is taking too long to appear and take care of the misery of his offspring. I would say then that spirituality (or more largely religion) has two distinct dimensions in your poetry: sometimes it is redemptive and other times it is portrayed as blind and unproductive faith, the opium that keeps people addicted, to use an old image.

Kei: Well, yes. But I think this sort of thing inevitably happens when we look closely at something and try to represent it fairly – it will resist being one dimensional. Don't get me wrong, the writer at times should represent things as being one-dimensional. There are truths in that as well, and for the sake of a good story, or a good poem, we can't afford to always be complicating things. That is much more an academic than an aesthetic impulse, to see things in their multi-nuanced, multilayered, complex ways. But I've written about religion far too often, and it means I've had to look at it through several angles. As I've said, my writing is in love with the Caribbean, and also with religion, but it doesn't try to be an apologetics for either.

Gloria: Your poetic expression cuts three distinct "models" of English: Standard English (for most poems in *Anger*), nonstandard English and patois. Judith Butler believes that "… the task is not simply to change language, but to examine language for its ontological assumptions, and to criticise those assumptions for their political consequences." If you agree to this proposition, then which is your language of creativity?

Kei: I've never attempted to understand Judith Butler before. Perhaps that's a kind of laziness. It's a great credit to you that you've chosen a quote that's at least half-discernible to me. But I think I might be a little lost with how you move from her proposition to this suggestion that I have to make, or that I have made a "choice" in language. Maybe I've misunderstood your question, but it seems to me that to ask a writer what is his language of creativity is like asking a pianist what is his "key" of creativity, as if he composed everything in C minor or E sharp. Surely it's the combination that makes it creative – the ability to slide from end of the piano to the next and

make a composition that creates harmony out of several keys. That is what the English Language is for me – a wide scale along which I can slide.

Gloria: Perhaps I have to put it more succinctly....

[O.M.G!]

Gloria: Yes, your writing shows that you have made a "choice". In your poetry, "patois" is the privileged language of "truth" and "identification" as shown in several interjections and utterances in both collections. Take "What the evangelist should have said" for instance, where the critique on preachers is matched by expressions in two models of English. Perhaps it is done unconsciously, but this privileging of "patois" over the Standard English "model" is indicative of the language you feel most comfortable with – the one you laugh and cry in. So let's go back, way back before the utterances and "sliding" on the scale of language, to moments of picturing and imagination during which many creative writers in multilingual situations (and your poetry indicates you as a member of this group), have admitted they "create" or "think /imagine" in a particular first language before they switch to another second and probably a world language of wider reach.

Kei: You have previously, and I'd say astutely, noted a couple interesting things about my second collection: you have pointed out that the register I have chosen in *There is an Anger* is much more Standard English than it is Creole. And you've also recognized that the poems in this collection at least appear to be more personal, poems about the self. So I wonder that it didn't occur to you that these two things might be related. You see, contrary to what you're informing me about myself, I can tell you that the language I laugh and cry in is actually English, though Creole is a register that is very much available to me and which I feel quite comfortable in. So I'm afraid your psychoanalysis is a little off here. And it would have been off (even if you were correct!) because you're suggesting that the language of the "self" is the same as the language of creativity, and this just isn't so.

On another point, while I may concede to you, the critic,

interpretations of my poetry that I myself did not see or intend, I'm not sure I agree that there is any single language of truth in my poems – or rather that one (patois) is privileged. For instance, do the seventeen poems in "The Broken" not declare a kind of truth, and declare it emphatically in what is much closer to Standard English? Do the nine poems in "In This Country" not also declare a truth in Standard English?

And finally, I do understand now the kind of poet you're describing. But that's not me. I don't create in any one language and then translate. As I've explained to you in another question, my poems start off as a "piece of language". And it grows from there! And that first piece will fall anywhere on the "scale" I previously described. So I cannot essentialize my "language of creation" in the way you are asking me to. The language I privilege in any individual poem will depend on the persona, the situation they are in, and the story the poem is telling.

Irene: There is in the poem "Speaking in Tongues" from *There is an Anger that Moves*, the idea that poetic language, with all its gibberish qualities and irrational intelligences speaking their ways, possesses a profound renovating energy, an energy that becomes like God itself, giving us tremendous pleasure and making our world look anew, as if we were just newborns still in awe with our surroundings. We could say that poetry is the medium that allows us to *reach* God: poetry is the magic incantation that will bring him/her to our souls… Being a poet myself or a writer of *highly* poetic fiction, I do share that same belief in the power of language, language that liberates and cleanses and makes us feel connected and transcend ourselves, as it were. Like Martin Heidegger has said in *Poetry, Language, Thought*, "Everyday language is a forgotten and therefore used-up poem, from which there hardly resounds a call any longer" and so the need to find a language that recaptures that "call", that *home*, where we can *dwell* in, where we can *be* and find meaning. In this poem, the women are presented as the ones who can create this language and the man does not seem to see any value in that language. Can you tell us how that poem came about and why the women are (again) the protagonists?

Kei: The seed of that poem is in the middle of it – "what is language

but a sound we christen?". I had that thought for a long time and I guess as often happens, the fiction, the poem, finally grew around it. And as the poem grew, it led me to other truths – that what I was doing as a poet, and what the woman caught up in religious ecstasy – in Pentecost – what we were doing were essentially the same things. We were throwing out sounds into the great out-there and trying to make sense of something much bigger than us.

The protagonists are women simply because it is what felt most natural, most authentic to the scene, to the fiction that I was describing. I guess it could have been men, but it wasn't. We make choices, and in this there were only two. Now, in my sequence of poems, Rum Bar Stories, there are hardly any women there at all; and it would have seemed an odd choice to force women into that space.

Irene: In both *The Kingdom of Empty Bellies* and *There is an Anger that Moves* we find abundance of Christian religious images and frequent recurrence to biblical figures and scenes. Were you raised in a very religious setting? Tell us about religion in Jamaica. Would it be fair to say that religion in Jamaica falls under the category of what some have called a syncretism of Christianity and Afro-rooted beliefs like in some parts of Brazil for instance?

Kei: I grew up in the church. It would be unfair to say that I was "raised" that way. My parents weren't as religious as I was. Eventually we didn't even go to the same church. They were Anglican and I found it really boring, because I was young and only wanted to go back home for breakfast. But eventually I left that church and of my own free will went to another. Religion in a way was always my own choice, though my parents, being reasonably religious, were happy with it, and subsequently they haven't been happy with my withdrawing from that space.

One part of Jamaica's religious landscape is the kind of syncretism you describe – Revivalism would be the prime example of this. But that's only one part of the landscape. Black nationalism takes the form of religion with Rastafari of course, and even some Nation of Islam; in Kumina and Obeah there is almost no Christian influence – just Africa; and then you have those Christian churches which are traditionally very

black, but not necessarily "Afro-rooted" – the Baptists, the Methodists, etc.

But Jamaica is incredibly religious and what almost all these religions might have in common – the Revivalists, Rastafarians, Obeah believers and of course Christians – is a huge regard and dependence on the Bible. The religions might exist along a broad spectrum, but the language of all of them is quite biblical.

Gloria: Could you expatiate on the idea that "in Kumina and Obeah there is almost no Christian influence – just Africa"? Here in Africa, there are hardly religious practices with such a name. Further, African traditional religion in practice till this date has had little or nothing to do with the Bible. On the contrary, the Pentecostal churches (Revivalists) which keep springing up at all corners, and the orthodox churches of Catholic and Anglican denominations, have yet to jettison traditional influences in their religious practices and ceremonies.

Kei: Yes – I should clarify and say that Obeah and Kumina represent not the reality of Africa, but our own imagination of it. They are, for us, a connection. They hold onto a lot of the ritual and even a lot of the language of Africa. Kumina in particular is a way to "travel" back to this land we've been separated from. But as I said, I'm not an Africanist, or an anthropologist. Other researchers more able and more interested than myself – Maureen Warner-Lewis and Olive Lewin for instance – have explored these connections in depth.

Gloria: Mary Osirim opines that "at the close of the twentieth century… the majority of women in English speaking Caribbean persist in unrewarding gender-segregated activities that severely restrict their upward mobility." Because the absence of "male voice" in your poetry is deafening, is religion one of such "unrewarding gender-segregated activities"?

[I should have asked her to clarify – was it a male voice that was missing from my poetry, or a traditionally masculine voice. The difference here may be subtle, but I think essential. Though the poems often privilege female subjectivity, they are almost always narrated by a male voice.]

Kei: It's too glib a statement for me. Religion is a space particularly

dominated by the woman. Religious ecstasy, which I so often describe, is often performed by the female subject. Would I go from there and say religion was "gender-segregated"? No. That's a very fixed position which is inevitably untrue. And "unrewarding" according to whom and by what standard? It seems you'd have to hold the religious subjects' belief in contempt to see it like that. Religious rhetoric of course rejects strictly capitalist notions of "reward". They will tell you they are storing up riches in Heaven – that their "measure has been pressed down, shaken together and is running over". And I have a deep respect for this belief.

Now Mary Osirim may well be right that "the majority of women in the English-speaking Caribbean persist in unrewarding gender-segregated activities that severely restrict their upward mobility". But the majority of people in the English-Speaking Caribbean persist in activities that restrict their upward mobility. The fact need not be gendered to be true. I'm also not sure what Osirim's take is on university education which you could just as easily argue is a "gender-segregated activity". The classroom, like the church, is a place where women are much more represented than men.

Irene: Your previous answer to Gloria's question again suggests that you are avoiding the political by not wanting to touch the issue of gender imbalance in the Caribbean. So I know that I am taking a risk here by asking you another of those questions that may irritate you. As I have said in a recent interview published in the last volume of *The African Journal of New Poetry*, from my personal experience and extensive academic investigation on what I call "The Patriarchies of Post-colonies", many black men (and I certainly don't mean to generalize) are often very sensitive about racial oppression and yet fail to see how oppressive and abusive they can be towards women, both black and white women, even though they may be much more oppressive towards black women. I have encountered this behaviour in black men living in North America (Canada and the United States), the Caribbean, South Africa and Mozambique to name but a few. There are of course many explanations for this behaviour and we could link it to internalized

oppression for example like Frantz Fanon did, and the need
the oppressed black man may have to oppress a perceived weaker
"other". Yet I must say I have little patience for a rhetoric that
justifies (excuses or underplays) oppression of another with
the internalized oppression of the oppressor since such rhetoric
only victimizes the oppressed and further emphasises the idea
that one can never exit the cycle of oppression, empathize with
the weak and always identifies with the power figure. I think
that in post-colonial societies there is a much greater concern
or impatience towards racial oppression than towards gender
oppression as if to be racist is a unforgiving sign (and it should
indeed be so) but being a patriarch (or a womanizer) is just
part of a naturalized system of male-female relations. There is
often a greater concern for the respecting of cultural differences
than for the respecting of women's rights. In Mozambique for
instance, polygamy is defended by many because it's seen as a
"true" African cultural tradition even though it is very detrimental
to women's rights and dignity. And now that I have spoken
my mind, and I apologize for my lengthy exposé, I ask you if
you could give me your perspective on this subject.

[This, of course, was a very well put rebuttal, and I'm not
certain that my response paid it as much attention as it was
due.]

Kei: Irene, I think you're quite right in all of this. I'm less certain
what "all of this" has to do with my poems. But it is a seriously
interesting and provocative question that you're raising. If
I may, I'd like to highlight another kind of example to answer
you in a somewhat circuitous way – the case of homophobia
in the Caribbean. This is territory which both my short-fiction
collection and my novel has gone into. It's a real problem
in Jamaica – the ku-klux-klan-like killing of homosexuals.
But does it not occur to me, at times, that a large part of
this issue is wrapped up in the way many Jamaicans resort
to aggression to solve any number of our problems, and that
violence becomes too easy a way for us to register our
disapproval of any number of things? Might it not occur to

me, on one random night, that Jamaica is probably no more homophobic than – say – small town America? Yet the expression of our homophobia is extreme. So tell me, what should the activist choose to address: Jamaica's homophobia, or Jamaica's violence? See, I do not believe that by acknowledging the broader problem of violence that affects everyone, that we have minimized the particular case of homosexuals who are certainly victimized. Again, tell me – what should the activist choose to address? My own position is: take your pick! They are both big things that really must be tackled. But I really must defend my right to sometimes look beyond the individual oppressions that of course are valid, and look on this greater picture, this wider context, and I don't think this is minimizing anyone's truth or the severity of any one problem.

The big point I am trying to make is simply this: in the Caribbean, in the whole world I am sure, there are many crosses we have to bear. Most of them are quite heavy. And all of them need bearing. But we need to stop expecting everyone to bear every cross. Goodison once said something that I really like: "we must all bring our own portion of light". I am sorry if sometimes my light does not shine on every issue equally, but it is what I bring.

Gloria: "Dreadlocks", "Bob Marley Music excerpts", "Sammy Dead" and all manner of cultural tropes abound in your poetry. Do these references reflect Rastafarian radicalism as an indigenous-styled communal identity that continues to reject the slave heritage and western imperialism till the present? Is there a great following for Rastafarianism in enlightened Caribbean cultures as yours?

[I should have pointed out: please, "Rastafari" – not "Rastafarianism". Rastafari don't believe in "isms".]

Kei: I think we've come back to the question of, what is my agenda? And I'll always resist declaring what that might be, beyond the ambition to simply write a good poem, or a good novel. On a basic level these references simply reflect the "where" of the poem. I've situated my poems in a Caribbean landscape,

in Jamaica specifically, so they naturally reach out to the culture that surrounds it, invoking Rastafari in one poem and Revivalism in another, and Reggae and Dancehall in others. But I hesitate to say the poem is a proponent of any of these things.

Rastafari is extremely visible and dynamic in Jamaica, and yet if you took a census of what religions people actually belonged to, Rastafari might seem to be a very small minority. Its influence is much, much bigger than its congregation.

Gloria: The way you "have learnt to stretch/ (your) nation" is interesting. What manner of transnationalism do you propose for the modern black condition of diasporic existences?

Kei: I don't think I want to propose any such thing, Gloria. That sounds dangerous. The diasporic subject is already quite capable of inventing his own very complicated ways of being – it is not something I could ever be prescriptive about, it is only something I observe – even marvel at.

Gloria: In *Anger*, the sense of loss catalyses most poems. This tends to verify the Freudian concept of "art and neurosis" which Julia Kristeva modifies by situating the creative art as a bye-product of depression...

[Do you notice that she wrote "by product" earlier, and now "bye-product". Is it very mean of me to recognize these misspellings?]

Gloria ...occasioned by "loss of ties, meaning" without which we would not call into question the stability of meaning, the banality of expression. How much anger motivates your poetry more than the usual themes of love and appreciation?

Kei: Off hand, I'd say very little. Emotions are hardly ever at the beginnings of my poems. I do believe that poetry, as a finished product, must swell with feelings – whether that be anger, or a poignant sadness, or triumph, or whatever really – but I'm not sure these feelings ever motivate me into poetry. What motivates me is an image I've thought of, or even more likely it is because I've found a small part of the language of the poem – and that little bit of language, that crumb, makes me hungry for the rest of it and so I work very hard to unravel the rest of that language.

Gloria: For most Africans, "writing itself is a political art" because
a writer "must be aware of the moral and political implications
of the characters involved in the story vis-à-vis global issues.
To what extent do you accept your poetry as political literature?
Secondly, should we interpret your nostalgia in *Anger* as patriotic
"positive presentations" of Jamaica which, in the opinion
of the Afrocentric scholar O.O. Enekwe, becomes another
method of "working against the racist stereotypes" found
in the West?

Kei: I have my own politics of course. To suggest otherwise would
be a very silly denial on my part. And I assume my politics
must come out in whatever I write. I imagine it will do this
quite naturally, because that's just the way I see the world.
And if, afterwards, my writing gets taken up by some group
or the other as a vehicle to propagandize these politics, these
truths as I see them, I would not be terribly sad. Indeed, it
would be a good thing. But I do not set out to write political
literature and I absolutely do not care for that label.

Gloria: Talking of influences and sources of inspiration, who are
your favourite writers and to what extent have earlier Caribbean
writers influenced your poetry?

Kei: I mentioned Lorna Goodison before who was a very big
influence on my poetry, and Olive Senior and Erna Brodber
who were influences on my fiction. But, of course, every writer's
genealogy is quite complicated; indeed, mine isn't restricted
to regional writers, nor is it in fact restricted to writers at all.
I draw on Emily Dickinson and W.S. Merwin, and Salman
Rushdie; I have drawn influence from certain preachers in
Jamaica, from certain artistes like Buju Banton, from snippets
of conversations I have heard on the bus...

But I must acknowledge that earlier Caribbean writers have
probably influenced my writing in ways I cannot tell or be
fully appreciative of yet. The problem with every younger
generation is that we walk very casually through doors that
have been wrenched open for us, not always understanding
we couldn't have this before. So there is a way in which the
Louise Bennetts and Earl Lovelaces and Linton Kwesi Johnsons
and my father's own godfather, Vic Reid – these people created

a space in which my own work now resides and makes sense and is read, and I give thanks to them for that.

Irene: In the section entitled "The Broken (1)" of the collection *There is an Anger that Moves*, you speak of breaking silence, of being you, of not hiding behind the "tall-hats" and the "coffins filled with johncrow feathers" which you refer to in *Kingdom of Empty Bellies*. You speak of loving what seems to be forbidden, you speak of breaking your mother's heart. Can you elaborate on what it is that you are in fact "breaking"?

Kei: Please don't think me rude if I say that if I thought the poem needed elaboration, then the poem would have been longer.

Irene: The section "The Broken (2)" is characterized by a powerful universal feel of suffering, vulnerability and the individual fragility of being. I find this section particularly beautiful. Here you speak of memory, love, hurt and loss, the un-expression of love (the difficulty in expressing it through words), the difficulty in showing love that feels like love at the moment it is being expressed. You speak of knowing and not knowing, of needing the other to know yourself and you also speak of knowing as something that you only understand intellectually in the future when remembering your past, like the love for your mother or for your lover. This love, as you seem to be saying, is the actual *being with* the other, the *being present and physical*, the *being in the moment*, the very stumbling that one experiences in our relations with other humans, and even though words may not be said, for we cannot find them right then, the actions of the present are the *actual* and *truest* acts of love, a love that may not be recognized by the intellect as such at that moment. Only the body (and perhaps the soul) can see *that love* in the moment it is being expressed. For the intellect it may feel as though the present, and *all the love* that it brings, is always incomplete, ephemeral, a stage when we are at a loss. And yet as you remind us here the present is complete: "the now is so large/the present is everywhere." It is in the present that *we are in fact wholly* and we are always in the present: "On that day we see each other./He undresses me. I say,/This is my body – and it is for you."

Kei: I am humbled that you like this poem, and that's a very generous reading of it. Thank you for giving me that.

Gloria: An interesting technique in your poetry is the use of what might be called "contrapuntal" ideas reminiscent of 17th century "wit" in English metaphysical poetry. In your case, not only do you import and combine the most unusual images at surprising moments, but you actually make the paradox conveyed by the images concur at the end. I notice this more in the poems in *Anger* collection than in *Bellies*. Is there any special reason for this? And, again, is there any particular influence in this direction?

Kei: Not sure I know where that kind of influence is coming from – perhaps it doesn't even come from a poetic antecedent, but rather from a kind of church sermon/prophetic culture that informs my aesthetics. I think I'm always gunning for a eureka moment: I want the end of the poem to climax in a way – to become a sort of epiphany.

Gloria: Thank you for giving us your time in this chat.

[I suspect what she meant to say was, I'm glad this is finally over.]

Kei: No – Thank you! For your provocative, and sometimes "provoking" questions. It was a pleasure.

[And what I meant to say was, I'm glad, too.]

RIFFING OF RELIGION
(Kenyon College, October 2012)

In the great wardrobe of the world there are, of course, many garments of religion, but those of us who at some point have chosen, or who still choose, to wear an ensemble from these racks, have tended to wear only one or two items – even if in time they wear thin in places or have to be mended in others. Yet we often make our own private faiths – our specific experiences of religion – synonymous with the entire wardrobe. I feel I must own up to that from the outset and acknowledge the limits of my religious experience, which is the world of Protestant Christianity in the Caribbean.

I should also start by giving thanks to you for coming out, and to the Department of Religious Studies, and to Professor Ennis Edmonds, in particular, for not only inviting me, but for putting up with me: I am by no means the easiest person to grab hold of by email, but people like Professor Edmonds generously forgive this as part of my artistic temperament. I also thank him for giving me a title. I had been writing down notes but had no idea of the title under which to collect them. As if divinely inspired (which, for this occasion, you must agree is quite fitting) Professor Edmonds provided me with the title to what I had already been writing – Riffing of Religion. I like the way the word "of" sits so strangely, as if it could just as well be "on" or "off" – both of which are completely appropriate, though the latter makes another echo – "Ripping off religion", which is maybe exactly what I am up to as well.

So I thought I would to describe to you how I came to church, and then how I left, because that journey has almost everything to do with how I came to writing and the things that I write about. But I will approach from a side door, and tell you first about a cousin of mine.

Coming and Going: I

About my cousin – let us call him Raymond – it would be
diminishing or even cheapening to describe him as merely "a gifted
musician". It is much truer to say that he has something that
approaches genius. He hears music from the inside out. He knows
what it can do and, more importantly, he knows how to make it
do those things. By training he is a classical pianist but he fell
out of that world completely – out of Mozart and Bach and Schubert
– and got himself involved in a Pentecostal church. As the family
whispers it, he had taken his parents' divorce hard and for him
church was – in all kinds of ways – a salvation. Being musically
inclined he began to write songs for the church, labelling himself
as no longer a mere pianist but in the high holy order of psalmist.
In fact, there was a chorus I used to sing in my own church when
I was growing up – "Sons of War Arise, Sons of War arise/From
the ends of the Earth arise/fire in your hands/fire in your mouths/
fire in your feet." I had always believed this song to be as old
and as unascribably authored as any other song we used to sing
in church, but in fact it had been written by my cousin.

Now Raymond tells me this strange and magical story: he goes on
a mission trip to Barbados and while he was practising on the piano,
which he did every day, someone listening would say, "You know,
there is just something about the way you play – something – that
puts me in the mind of George." Over and over he would hear this.
"There is just something about the way you play – something – that
puts me in the mind of George."

George, it turned out, had once been a guitarist, of whom it would
also be a diminishing to say he was merely "gifted". Rather, he was the
kind of musician of whom it is truer to say, he had something which
approached genius. But like many artists of genius before him,
George had lost his mind. When Raymond arrived in Barbados,
George was living on the streets – his daily meal scavenged out of
garbage bins.

Now while people were telling my cousin about George, they
were also stopping in the street and telling George about Raymond.
"Boy, it have a man who staying up by the church who play piano, and
something bout the way he play put me in the mind of you."

Inevitably, the day comes when George and my cousin meet. It is the last day of the crusade. My cousin enters the auditorium from one door and George enters from another. They see each other and somehow (my cousin insists on this), they know each other. They simply know. The two men walk to the stage, my cousin sitting at the piano and George, for the first time in years, picking up a guitar. They begin to play a song – a song that my cousin describes as the most incredible thing he has ever played. The song lasts for almost two hours. In it, my cousin asked questions and George, following the riff and rhythm and rhyme of the music, provided answers. This spontaneous song was then a conversation between the two men in which the story of a life was told – of gifting and music and insecurities and falling away and voices in the head and psychic fragmentations. You must think here of the woman who touches the hem of the saviour's garments and tells him the WHOLE story of her life – no doubt talking for hours and hours. At the end of the song, George falls to the floor and weeps, and after that he is healed completely – his mind restored unto himself.

And with a logic I have never quite understood, my cousin narrates this encounter with the miraculous as a reason why he left the church, as if we must imagine the two men not only walking towards each other but also past and beyond each other – each one leaving out of the opposite door from which they had entered, so that George re-enters the church, and my cousin re-enters the world. I think I understand now that my cousin was really seeking other similarly profound encounters with the spiritual, which are not always found in religious spaces.

Coming and Going: II

When I entered religion it was to a church very similar to the one my cousin had been part of. This then was the charismatic world of pentecost, of speaking in tongues, of getting slain in the spirit. As a proper middle-class Jamaican boy I was always slightly outside of this world. I had grown up in an environment that maps much more closely onto a conservative white secularism (if not cynicism) rather than onto the world of black religious ecstasy.

Standing on the outside – the "outskirts" as I put it in one poem – meant that to some extent I was always observing and taking notes. Unknown even to myself I was being formed as a writer – listening closely to especially talented pastors and self-proclaimed prophets and prophetesses was a lesson in rhythm and in cadence, a lesson in how to combine images to cause surprise, or how to apply dissonant verbs to unlikely nouns so that the noun ended up doing something it had not done before, or how to completely free words from the cement of semantic conventions, so that they no longer meant what they were accustomed to mean, but were able to cause an experience, or even to be the experience. This was all the stuff of poetry. As well, I was gathering material, collecting images – the way a woman tilts her head or shivers in the presence of that which she understands to be holy, the way she spins away from the pulpit, her skirt filling like a sail or looking like a blossoming flower.

To imagine myself on the outskirts looking in implies a sort of a fence, a border between two worlds. It is a crude binary to create, yet I don't feel I have ever left that boundary place. It has felt like my burden to insist on the intellectual integrity of religious experience to those who tend to be more atheistically inclined, and to insist on the moral and ethical integrity of secularism and atheism to those who are more religiously inclined. These are the margins I try to bring to the centre of both worlds.

But why did I leave?

At the time it didn't feel like leaving, it was so slow a process. When I was seventeen or eighteen and was asked to give a series of talks at a summer camp, I was excited by the task. By then I had listened to enough sermons and felt it was something I could do. I spent a lot of time on those sermons, building my words carefully, constructing images in surprising ways, and then purposely deconstructing what had been built. I understood how sermons moved by ebb and flow, before at last, with one final tidal surge, they threw their listeners onto a specific shore.

I do not want to revel in the success of those sermons, and what they caused. Suffice to say they were successful. And after everything, after every song had been played, after everyone had cried themselves raw, after all was said and done, there were a series of hands on my shoulders and the gentle words: *God really used you today.*

It was a strange compliment to receive, because though I believed then as I believe now in the experience I had helped to create – which is the experience of feeling broken, or of being connected to one's brokenness, to one's frailty, and then feeling affirmed in that weakness – I understood it as an artistic construction, a crafted encounter with the self. I was beginning to free experiences such as these from the dogma in which others would want to firmly ground them. Though it would take a few years yet, just like my cousin, it was as if this connection to the somewhat miraculous spurred me on and out through the door – spat me back out into the secular world, which had now become the world in which we (my cousin and I) could recognize and seek out other spiritual experiences.

If in my journey I have left behind something of the dogma of church, what I did not leave behind was my notebook – those furious and detailed notes I had been taking for so long. And I didn't leave behind the respect I had for belief and the practice of belief and this obviously has become a theme of mine.

The thing about losing your religion

I have discovered that there is a way we lose our religion; we lose it in the way a child might lose an expensive watch in the playground, the very watch he was not supposed to take to school in the first place. He will not admit to having lost it at first. He will be too busy searching desperately. Days later, the moment will come that the child has been dreading. His mother will ask him, "Where is the nice watch your uncle gave you for Christmas?" The child will feel a sickness growing in his stomach; he will begin to wring his arms. "It is in my drawer," he will say at last, or, "I lent it to a friend." He is buying time. He is still hoping to find the watch again, that it will miraculously reappear. And this is how we lose our religion, by pretending we haven't lost it for a while – by searching high and low, or by saying it is upstairs in the bedroom drawer. And this kind of thing can go on for years.

The thing about losing your religion – if, like me, you grew up with friends who shared that religion – is that you suspect you are about

to lose something that lives in the middle of these friendships. You do not worry about losing the friendships themselves; they go deep enough and will survive in one form or another. It is the new form that you worry about. Understanding all too well the nature and the intensity of belief, you understand that the only way your friends can continue to love you is by pitying you, by feeling a little sorry for what you have become. They do not mean to be condescending; it is simply part and parcel of the religion they have and which they want to share as part of their love for you.

You know this because you used to do the same thing, too; you used to look on people who, it was whispered, had once been "on fire" (this was the kind of language you used when you had religion; it is yet another thing you have lost), who had become "lukewarm", neither hot nor cold, as having something worthy only of being spat out. How careless, how sad, for them to have lost something so precious as their fire!

And if some of your friends are now condescending towards you, you are every bit as condescending towards them. It shames you, this attitude you are able to detect in yourself, but each time you listen to a conversation in which the worst banalities of the language that you have lost are used, you cannot help but shake your head and roll your eyes. Whenever an old friend writes to say of a recent trip, "Events were well attended, and the blessed gospel was shared, and we are confident that God's Word will accomplish what He intends for it to accomplish", or that "on the days we have good weather, I enjoy the beauty of the Lord in the beauty He has created. What a gift!" you cannot help but smirk in disdain. This is why you wonder about your friendships, and the love that is between you, a love now undergirded by mutual contempt.

The thing about losing your religion is that you must come face to face with the thing you had previously learnt to avoid: the fact of death. And not just any death, but your own. For death can seem a great unfairness to us obsessed by our living (and it is easy to do this), conscious of our breaths, our unfolding possibilities, and of our uncertain allotment of tomorrows. To occasionally remember that each of these – breaths, possibilities and tomorrows – will run out one day causes a coldness in our bones. You could say this coldness is a taste of the death to come, but of course we won't in fact taste death.

The anticipation is undoubtedly worse than the thing itself; the dead do not waste time being angry that they are dead.

Now my mother saw her death coming towards her for years. She tried to avoid it but it finally caught her. She felt the death in her feet at first. In the last three days of her dying she called to say she could no longer feel them, but that her mouth was strong, and that she wished she could transfer some of the power from her voice to her feet. Because death caught my mother by her feet, she was not able to run away from it any longer, and because it had not yet reached her mouth, she was able to cry out that this horrible thing was happening to her. There had been days during those several years in which she was dying that I heard her in her room. She kept on saying, "Why me, Jesus?" I thought she had been asking, "Why do I have to be so ill at this age when all of my friends are still working?" But I think she was also asking something larger: "Why do I have to die, why does it have to end for any of us? Why do I have to lie in this bed and see this thing slowly coming towards me?" This is why her question was addressed to Jesus, because it would have been too horrible if death was simply coming to her, and there was nothing on the other side of it. Maybe this is why so many of us hold on to religion, because it is a blessing to walk towards death with your back always turned to it. When you lose your religion, in your attempts to find it again, you turn around and see the things you never wanted to see.

Maybe this is why there is a kind of atheist – the very evangelical kind (for atheists are sometimes more evangelical than believers) – who is usually deeply depressed, because he or she knows that only in death is religion really proved or disproved – which means that they will never get the chance to gloat and say, *I told you!* They must also suspect that even if they are right, it does nothing to invalidate a life that was filled with faith and joy and fulfilment and song.

The thing about losing your religion is that no one guesses how many times over how many years you have been down on your knees and spoken to the floorboards; they do not guess how many nights over how many years you have woken up and walked out into the night and spoken to the darkness; they do not guess how many times your head has fallen into your own hands and you have spoken to your palms – how desperately you have waited and listened, hoping that this time – this time – the silence really would respond, and you

could be convinced that the voice that came back was not of your own conjuring. Many would rather think that you have lost your religion through carelessness and they will pity you for your clumsiness and bad luck.

The strange thing, however, about losing your religion is that it does not diminish your capacity to believe. So you believe whole-heartedly in very odd things. You might believe in the pursuit of truths – however painful they may be – though this is not at all a strange thing to believe in, and everyone believes that they believe in this. You believe in love and will be sad at how much the world lacks it. You might believe in the colour orange, in taffeta and silk, in triangular plates, in the perfect sauce, in planes, in saying thank you, in the holding of hands, in light bulbs, in machetes, in keys (especially those from the 18th century), in Prague, Jerusalem and every city you have been to, and in water – and that in each of these there is a kind of magic, a kind of redemption. And so when you think deeply about each of these things, it can break you so utterly, in the way a pianist and a mad guitarist might break each other, or in the ways a good sermon used to orchestrate an encounter with your deepest self.

A SPACE BETWEEN THE POEMS: AN ATTEMPT AT A BENEDICTION

Written for the National Association of Literature Development Conference, "The Spaces Between Us". March 27, 2012

I was asked to write a poem for this event. This isn't one. Instead, it is my attempt at a benediction. Although it isn't a poem, it is about poems, and the reading of them at events such as this. I want to suggest what can happen in the spaces between poems, but also I'd like to tell you a little about those spaces in which I first found poetry.

I came to the genre later than other poets. There is no journal to be found that betrays me working out any teenage angst. Back then I was writing stories. I considered myself a writer long before I thought of poetry as a viable shape that writing might take. One semester at the University of the West Indies, the course on Creative Writing Prose was not being offered so I settled on the course on poetry. There, under the tutelage of Mervyn Morris, I began to learn the rules of this new genre. I did not do exceptionally well on the course, but the bug had bitten. When I left the space of university altogether (I dropped out), I did not leave the space of writing or poetry.

The new millennium had just started and we were all logging on to the new world of the internet. There I found an online poetry community called *Alsop Review*. I still think of it as my most important workshop experience. Other poets who I met online at that time and in that space include the English poet Frances Leviston and Angela France and the Caribbean poets Nicolette Bethel and Millicent Graham, and George Ttoouli who would one day help to found Heaventree Press. The workshop experience online was markedly different from the one at UWI for, as you might appreciate, when

people are separated by miles and by timezones, and when they are not disadvantaged by seeing actual faces and how those faces might break upon receiving bad news, then people will find the freedom to say things that they might not otherwise say, or which, in another context, they might say more gently. At the *Alsop Review* there were some who felt that to preserve high standards bad poets should be made to feel unwelcome.

When I posted my first poem there were definitely some people who decided I belonged to that category of poets or poetasters who should be made unwelcome. One man wrote a simple but eloquent instruction, "Fuck off." Another was more helpful, but equally vicious, "Go and read Four Quartets before you ever post here again!"

I wasn't shooed away so easily. I never left that group until I felt I had impressed them, or at least earned their respect. I still think it was this group, probably more than my future editors, that virtually edited my early work and thus, my first book. There is, of course, something being said here about the kinds of approval and validation I have sought, not always from the communities whose language I use and to whom I am writing most directly – as if I exist in a space between.

When I heard the Slam poet and activist Staceyann Chin read for the first time at the Calabash Festival in Jamaica (the first one), I knew my craft would be forever changed by that experience. I probably knew as well, as with the poetry of Lorna Goodison, that it would be an influence I would try to bury because its impact was so profound. I began to seek not only pages to write on, but stages where the work could find its best sounds. There certainly were those who hailed me as a new performance poet. It was a label which I hadn't yet grown completely uncomfortable with.

When I arrived in Manchester, England in 2004 to pursue an MA in Creative Writing, I arrived the way most students arrive – poor, and in my case without a scholarship or grant, and as yet without the money from the sale of my Nissan Lucino in Jamaica. Let me tell you now about the mechanics of a miracle. In that first penniless fortnight I saw posters around the city advertising an upcoming poetry festival. My heart leapt at the £100 prize that was going to be given out to a lucky poet who went on stage and captured the judges' hearts. I called

immediately to book a spot but was disappointed to find that all the spots were gone. I could only give them my name; they would put it in a box from which they would randomly pick and call names on the night. So, only if I was lucky...

There was yet another complication. The event started at 7:00 p.m. My class on Wednesdays also started at 7:00. I would have to rush from school, arrive late, and see if I was STILL lucky. It seemed at best that I would get to check out the Manchester poetry scene. Emerging from class at 8:30, I took a bus into the city centre, consulted a map and finally found my way to the club. Things were already wrapping up. Three of the four finalists had already been chosen. The box was empty but for one name. As I walked in they pulled out this last name and tried desperately to pronounce it: Key? Kay? Kei? Kei Miller?

My own name. My own name had waited for me. It had dodged every finger dipping into that box. It had sat at the bottom, clung to the cardboard, and waited until the body whose presence it spoke for had arrived. I went on stage and half an hour later I had won the competition. The next morning the newspaper reported it: Kei Miller, freshly arrived from Jamaica, had become the 2004 "Manchester Slam Poetry Champion".

I was deeply grateful for the money. I feel ungrateful to now admit to that small part of me that was ashamed to have won. It is not so strange a thing, perhaps, to feel shame on the one hand, and to feel ashamed of your shame on the other. It must be part of my Christian upbringing – this way of fanning the flames of guilt. Still, when Michael Schmidt of Carcanet, who was then my professor (of fiction), congratulated me, having read the news that I had won the city's slam competition, I knew that he was only being polite. However, it was the start of our friendship; it was how he discovered I was interested in poetry at all. Later on when I sent him some of my work, and he was convinced that my poems could hold their place on page as well as on the stage, I would become a Carcanet poet, and maybe this would not have happened if I hadn't slammed my way onto the page.

The debate I'm trying to reinvoke here is of course an old one, but one that shows no signs of dying down – the craft of poetry as it exists in rowdy performance halls versus the craft as it still exists in solitude;

a fight between the poet who does his best work standing up and finds his greatest eloquence on stage, or the poet who does his best work sitting down and who finds his greatest eloquence on page.

Tensed between these two poles I admit to having become the ultimate performance poet – for many times I have approached lecterns with blank white pages which I pretend to read from, or else I open my book at random places and read poems that are not actually on the page before me. I know my poems by heart, and even large passages from my novels, so the book or the page functions only as a prop that insists to my audience that my work is rooted on the page and that I am much more than a performance poet. But what does that mean? Is a performance poet necessarily inferior to a "page poet"? Once again, I find myself wondering about the places, the institutions, the audiences, the publishers and critics from whom I seem to be seeking validation.

It was a much more recent reading in Manchester – eight years after my slam poetry victory – that made me think more about these things – about the spaces in which I have created poetry, and the spaces I try to create between poems.

When I give a reading what I ultimately want to do is to move my audience in some way. It does occasionally happen, however, that it is the audience, instead, that moves me much more than I am able to move them.

The first time such a thing happened was in Jamaica. I had read in an auditorium where the rows of chairs ascended from the stage and so one had to look up into the audience. At the end of a poem there was this woman who rose magnificently from her seat, descended the stairs and at the edge of the stage paused in front of me. She lifted up her hand, kissed the palm of it, and then placed the palm solidly on the floor before my feet. And then, just as simply, she returned to her seat. A move so elegant, a vote of thanks so eloquent, it caused something larger than words to grow in my throat. It was difficult to continue that reading.

The prepared poet will have some kind of set list for a reading, might even practice reading the poems – aloud or in the quiet of his or her mind. An even more accomplished poet might consider and prepare, just as diligently, the spaces between the poems.

In these spaces, the poet often talks – though sometimes he might

be silent in a dramatic sort of a way, or make some kind of gesture. The point is, we move away from the script on the page and make another kind of contact with the audience. Sometimes, though, the lights on stage are so bright and the dark so envelops the audience that we cannot actually see anyone; we speak then to shadows and to silhouettes, which, in a way, is not dissimilar to the way we write.

In the spaces between poems we might tell the larger stories of our poems, of their beginnings, and also stories of ourselves. There are some who insist on never using such spaces, and others who use too much, until the spaces become larger than the actual poems. I confess to an unnatural fear of poets of a certain age who approach lecterns with a pair of spectacles hung around their necks and who bring these spectacles up to their eyes as if they are about to read, but who pull them away just before the first syllable of the poem, to say something else to the audience. This teasing game can go on for a very long time, so that audiences hold their breaths each time the spectacles approach the eyes, wondering if finally... finally... might we have the poem now?

The more often a poet gives readings, the more likely he is to use the spaces between poems in the same way. He will end up telling the same stories; he will pretend, as if randomly, to remember the same odd detail, and always in the same place. Even his body will repeat the same gestures – his hand rising or falling or flailing in exactly the same places. For this reason a poet might feel nervous, or found out, if he notices someone in the audience who has attended a previous reading. The poem is scripted; the audience appreciates this fact. But the audience would like to believe that the spaces between poems are unscripted, spontaneous, meant specially for them in that specific moment.

I will admit to one rehearsed gesture that I have noticed myself doing at almost every reading. When I read from the collection *A Light Song of Light*, I usually end with the long poem that comes closest to being the title poem. It is called "Twelve Notes Towards a Light Song of Light".[1] From the title you can guess at the structure of the poem – twelve parts, small poems really, each one suggesting how this "light song of light" might behave, what a "light song of light" may or may not do. When I get to the last note, the twelfth small poem as it were, I usually close the book. I look out to the audience as if I am no longer reading a poem, as if (in fact) I have moved into a space

between the poems, as if I am addressing each person specifically, as if the moment is unscripted. And then I say the line, "A Light Song of Light says thank you".

What I want is for my audience to feel the linebreak, the enjambment. I want them to understand that I am in fact saying to them, *Thank you – thank you for listening to me – for sitting down for so long and being lovely – thank you for being patient and attentive and receptive.* And I want them to understand this before the poem moves on to its next line and explains that it is actually thanking "the paper it is written on/ this most solid evidence of its existence".

This was the final poem I read a few nights ago in Manchester and I read the above line in the way I have just described. And then something happened.

Before I could move beyond the linebreak, to the next explaining line, three women stood up. They had made their own way into a space between the poem and the listener, and like a triumvirate of goddesses they clasped their hands and nodded towards me. It was a nod so deep that it was almost a bow. I was aware of these women's blackness. I was aware that they looked like my mother. I knew at once that these women probably spoke with my mother's accent. I was aware that I had been writing poems that depicted them but had not necessarily sought their approval, and here they were willingly giving it to me.

I faltered. Something larger and more emotional than words was swelling in my throat. These women had not only moved into the space between poems, but they had expanded it. It was now their space. It was they who were holding me in it. Because I was on the verge of crying, I made myself look on the floor until the moment passed and I could complete the poem.

Perhaps these are the kinds of spaces that writers and curators and literature developers are always trying to create – spaces that exist outside the actual words, outside the actual events – in which people are able to live and breathe and move and think and have their beings. We are gathered here tonight as developers of literature, and I wonder if perhaps these are the kinds of spaces we must always be conscious of creating, or trying to create, whether they exist online, or on the page, or in physical auditoriums. May I suggest that we must always be desirous of creating spaces in which

people might meet themselves, and know themselves, and celebrate themselves, and are even able to say back to us: thank you for giving ourselves back to us, because sometimes in this world we have had to live without our selves for long stretches of time.

I left that most recent reading in Manchester and went outside to a group who had stayed back to wait for me. They invited me back to a house in Chorley where a man named Winston prepared an extravagant feast for this spontaneous midnight gathering. There was ackee and saltfish and callaloo and roasted breadfruit and sweet potatoes. There was a table of coca cola and rum and vodka. In all, there were maybe twenty people who had come over from the reading and in the front room of that house in Chorley we all sat down and I mostly listened to their stories. I was laughing and crying until five o'clock that morning. And although it was not my house, and although I had no hand in the cooking of the food, or in the buying of the rum, I would like to believe that I helped to create that space. It was a space between poems and between people, in which we were able to meet again.

And in saying all of this, you must realize, I am trying to create such a space even now.

End Note

1. Actually, it's called "Twelve Notes FOR a Light Song of Light", but if I were to reissue the book now I'd change that "for" to "towards".

INDEX

ABOUT THE AUTHOR

Kei Miller is a poet, novelist and essayist. He was born in Kingston, Jamaica where he grew up and still spends much of his time. Kei did an MA in Creative Writing at Manchester Metropolitan University and then a PhD in English Literature at Glasgow University where he is now Reader and Director of the Creative Writing programme. His work has been shortlisted for a number of international awards including a Dylan Thomas Prize, a Commonwealth Writers First Book Prize, and a John Llewelyn Rhys Prize. His novel, *The Same Earth*, won Jamaica's Una Marson Prize and he has received a Silver Musgrave Medal from the Institute of Jamaica. In 2013 the Caribbean Rhodes Trust awarded him the Rex Nettleford Fellowship in Cultural Studies.